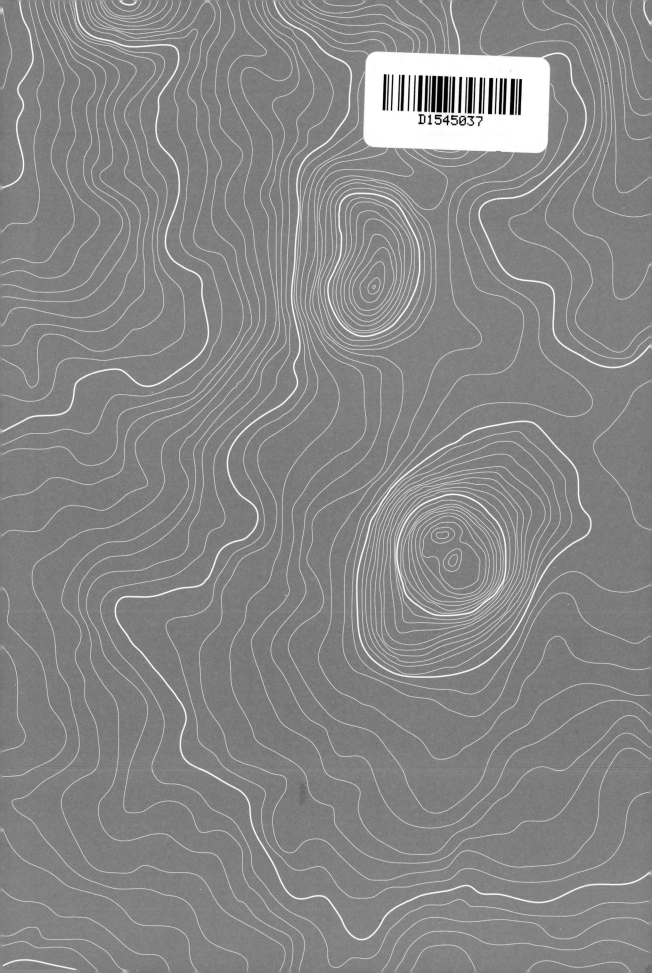

ATLAS OF VANISHING PLACES

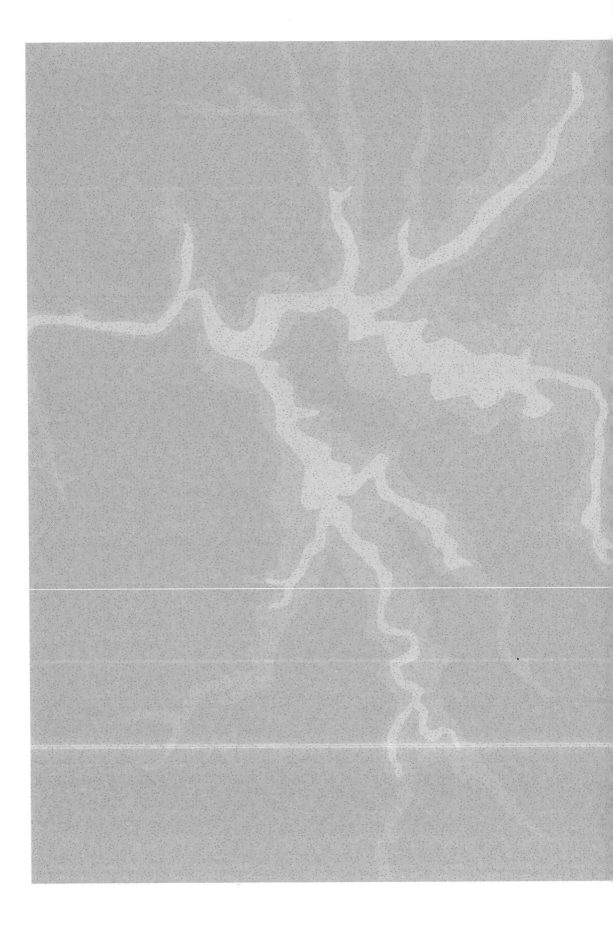

ATLAS OF VANISHING PLACES

THE LOST WORLDS AS THEY WERE AND AS THEY ARE TODAY

TRAVIS ELBOROUGH

MAPS BY MARTIN BROWN

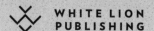

WHITE LION PUBLISHING

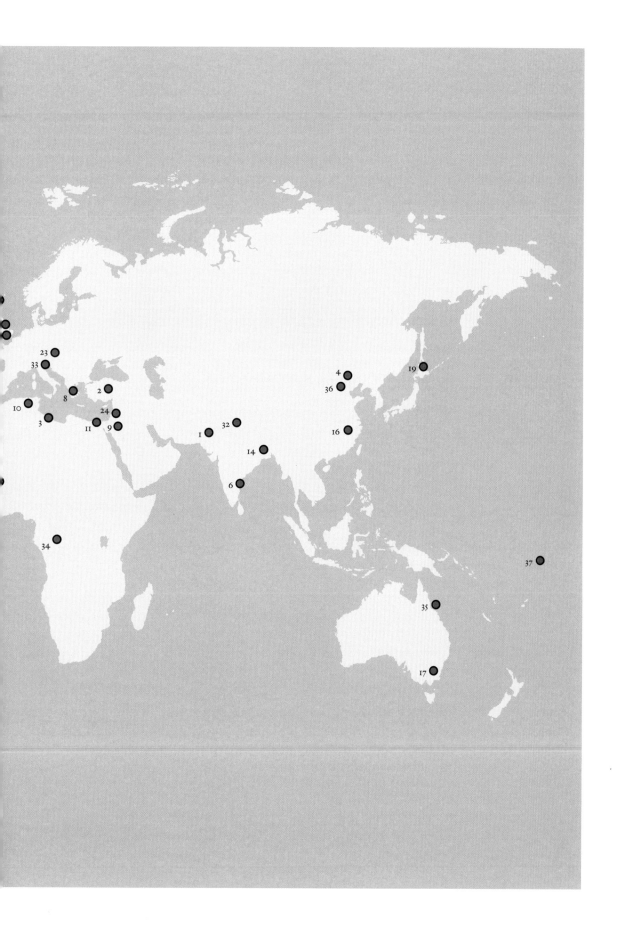

SHRINKING PLACES

THREATENED WORLDS

INTRODUCTION

The word 'vanish' in English, meaning 'to go, disappear or cease to exist', derives from the Old French *esvanir*, which in turn comes from the Latin *evanescere* (to evaporate), a phrase we most readily associate with departing liquids. The roots of this volume arguably lie in the story of the demise of the Aral Sea in Uzbekistan, related in an earlier book, *Atlas of Improbable Places.* The Aral was once the fourth largest lake in the world; its waters teemed with enough flounder, catfish and saltwater carp to supply a sixth of the fish eaten across the whole of the USSR. But the decision taken in the 1950s to divert two of the region's main rivers, the Amu Darya and the Syr Darya to irrigate land for cotton production radically reduced the amount of water flowing to the Aral Sea. Between 1960 and 1996, its water levels dropped by some 16m (52½ft). By 2007, the sea had shrunk to 10 per cent of its original size and where fish had previously swum and trawlers bobbed about on the saline swell of the Aral's waves there were now only dry expanses of salty sand, much of them riddled with harmful pollutants. There is little hope of restoring the Aral and its tragic fate is a direct consequence of deliberate human intervention in the local environment. If an extreme example, it is nevertheless indicative of the broader and unintended effects that our actions are having more generally on the planet. The evidence of what our continued dependency on fossil fuels and exploitation of scarce natural resources are doing to the world is plain to see. And all but scientifically irrefutable. Landscapes lost, or at least severely depleted, due to climate change induced rises in sea levels and altered weather patterns, unavoidably, and sadly necessarily, provide many of the entries in this atlas, a gazetteer of sorts, to places gone and going.

Here too, nevertheless are ancient sites and spaces that were erased from the maps in half-forgotten times past, only to resurface again – if usually, only as shadows of their former selves or as mere ruins. In either case, they inevitably serve as totems for the vanished civilizations and societies that first created them. Their very lost-ness is intrinsic to any kind of unearthing and resurrection they might subsequently have come to enjoy. And being found is part of the means for us to discover just how much, or what, has been mislaid over the centuries.

Old maps, though, can provide us with the chance to do a spot of time travel, journeying as our ancestors might have done through cities, kingdoms and whole empires that no longer exist. In some instances the charts are all that remain of the territories, their precise coordinates no longer mapping onto any recognizable part of the world today. Maps can also be a means for mourning, pored over wistfully, sometimes painfully, for what once was, and read as an act of remembrance for an irretrievable place and its former inhabitants.

More usually we look at maps to decide where to go in the future. They are often the first points of departure for somewhere new and more interesting, somewhere with different, and hopefully better, food, weather and scenery. And our internet-aided present puts once entirely unknown and enticing locations at our fingertips, only increasing, if anything, our appetites for places eerie, untouched and abandoned in the process. Distances in time and space are distorted beyond anything previously imagined in earlier cartography; on digital maps such as Google Earth the sense of global interconnectivity is palpable. And yet despite helping to make decayed buildings and cities highly Instagram-able, the actual physical reality of the earth's immense and current and ever-pressing fragility can seem rather oddly intangible online. The screen and the swipe, if showing us more of the world, can somehow simultaneously shield us from the truth about its increasing vulnerability. What follows on tactile paper and in print, and through words and pictures, if even perhaps accessed digitally, is a survey of landscape and locations transformed by circumstances, some much disputed, or improbable and entirely unexpected; others, depressingly, almost grimly predictable. As such it ideally serves as a reminder of the mutability of existence but also a clarion call for the urgency of preserving what we hold dear for generations to come.

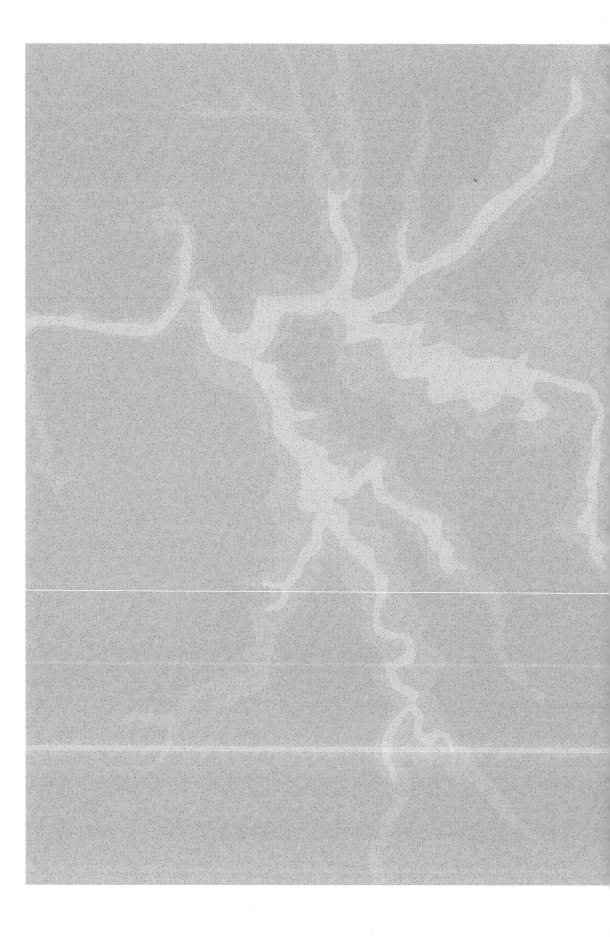

ANCIENT CITIES

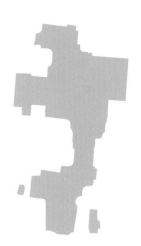

MOHENJO-DARO

PAKISTAN

27° 19′ 27.4″ N / 68° 08′ 07.5″ E

Until the 1920s, when R.D. Banerji, an officer of the Archaeological Survey of India, began excavating a site on the banks of the Indus river in what today is the northern Sindh province of Southern Pakistan, the world remained oblivious to the existence of an entire ancient civilization, quite possibly the equal of that of Egypt and neighbouring Mesopotamia. A century earlier a British explorer named Charles Masson had turned up some mysterious brick mounds in the area, fragments, as it subsequently emerged, of the lost city of Harappa, but failed to delve any further. Engineers laying the railway through the region in the 1850s viewed the arcane stone work they encountered as a nuisance impeding the progress of the line. Being of a practical and pragmatic mindset, that didn't stop them carrying the bricks off as souvenirs or repurposing them in other building work along the way. But following the example of Howard Carter, a pioneer of modern scientifically systematic archeological excavations, who was digging for Tutankhamun's tomb in the Valley of the Kings, Banerji and his colleagues' hunch that there might be something more to these curious stones than many first supposed was vindicated almost immediately.

What they found were the remnants of not one but two lost cities, Harappa and its larger sibling Mohenjo-Daro. The latter, whose name is taken to mean 'mound of the dead' was eventually revealed to extend for a circuit of 3 miles (5km) and is believed to have been the epicentre of an exceedingly advanced civilization that flourished beside the Indus in 2500–1700 BC. With a series of mounds and baked-brick buildings arranged along an orderly grid scheme, possessing a sophisticated drainage system and boasting a great public bath located on the largest mound, Mohenjo-Daro offers an astonishingly early example of

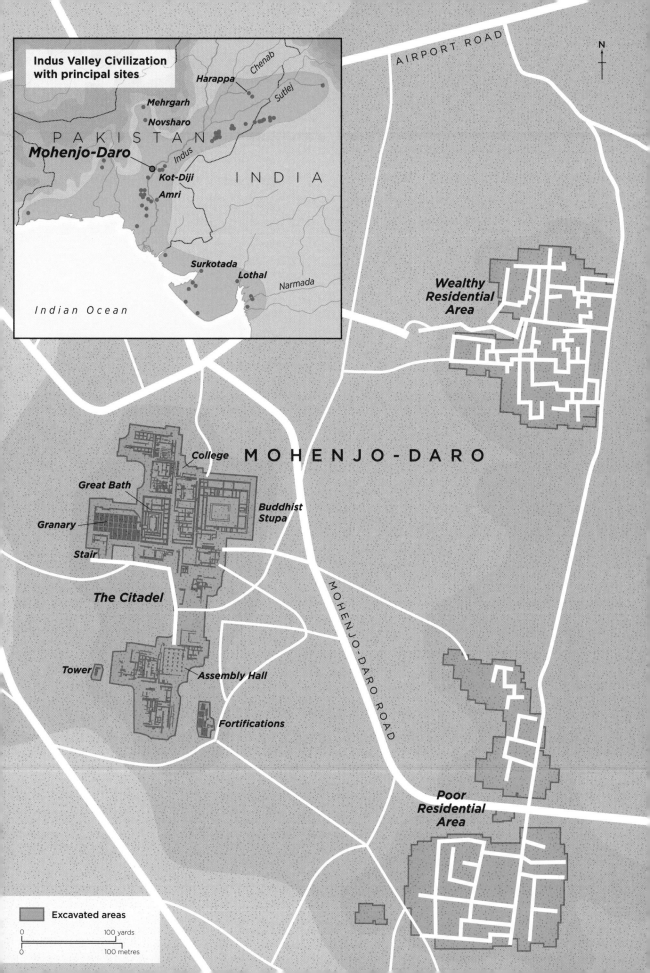

Indus Valley Civilization with principal sites

Harappa
Chenab
Mehrgarh
Sutlej
Novsharo
P A K I S T A N
Mohenjo-Daro
Indus
Kot-Diji
I N D I A
Amri

Surkotada
Lothal
Narmada

Indian Ocean

AIRPORT ROAD

N

Wealthy Residential Area

M O H E N J O - D A R O

College

Great Bath

Buddhist Stupa

Granary

Stair

The Citadel

Tower

Assembly Hall

Fortifications

MOHENJO-DARO ROAD

Poor Residential Area

Excavated areas

0 — 100 yards
0 — 100 metres

hygienic urban planning – an all-mod-cons metropolis dating back at least 4,500 years.

The society that created and occupied this city evidently cared about cleanliness and health. Its people were clearly very wealthy, as evidenced by the richness of pottery, gold, lapis and ivory artefacts, and the shattered sections of delicately carved statuary recovered, as well as the scale of the buildings. But its citizens didn't go in for quite the same degree of out-and-out gaudy ostentation as some of their near peers in the ancient world, with regal palaces and temples conspicuous by their absence.

What manner of people they truly were continues to puzzle archaeologists and anthropologists. As, naturally, does exactly how and why this civilization fizzled out entirely, leaving its epic cities abandoned and lost for so long. Among the grimmer discoveries at Mohenjo-Daro are forty-four skeletons who appear to have perished in the city's streets during some single violent event. What killed them, however, will most likely never be known. The once popular theory that the city was the victim of a great flood has largely been discounted now. But others believe that a definite shift in the course of the Indus river might well have been the event that precipitated its decline.

RIGHT: The archaeological site of Mohenjo-Daro, in the province of Sindh, Pakistan.

BELOW: Significant excavation work has been conducted at the site of the city, which was designated a UNESCO World Heritage Site in 1980.

HATTUSA

TURKEY

40° 00' 39.1" N / 34° 36' 56.9" E

A great people known as the Hittites are mentioned throughout the books of the Hebrew Tanakh (Old Testament) and usually in some context as worthy, if troublesome, adversaries of the Israelites and their God. And yet until the nineteenth century these few isolated Biblical references to the Hittites were all historians of the ancient world had to go on. They appeared to have evaded the attention of every other scribe going and there remained not so much as a broken piece of pottery from their apparently vast empire left in the lands of the Middle East or across the Mediterranean. Having seemingly disappeared without trace, doubts persisted about their very existence. After all, how could a people spoken of in the same breath as the mighty Assyrians and Babylonians just vanish off the face of the earth? Were they merely the result of a Canaanite misattribution, or the clumsy slip of a Talmudic clerk's pen or chisel?

The case for a Hittite Empire, however, was bolstered after the discovery in 1799 of the Rosetta Stone by Napoleonic troops in Egypt. This was the key to deciphering hieroglyphics, and it was found that ancient Egyptian texts were littered with accounts of their run-ins with the Hittites. Their records recounted one especially epic battle between the armies of King Ramses II of Egypt and the Hittite King Hattusilis III in around 1279 BC on the borders of present-day Syria and Lebanon. However self-serving the Egyptian version of events possibly were, they left no doubt that the Hittites were an advanced and powerful people whose kingdom covered swathes of the middle and near east, which, frankly, in the face of the continuing absence of any mark of their time on earth, now only made their complete erasure even more baffling.

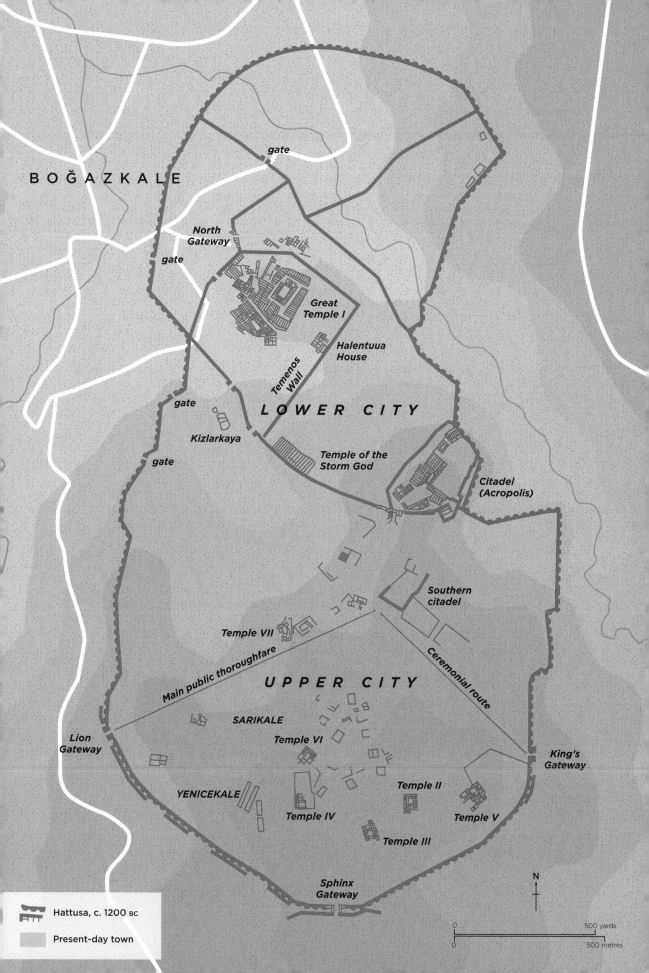

BOĞAZKALE

gate

North
Gateway

gate

Great
Temple I

Halentuua
House

Temenos Wall

LOWER CITY

gate

Kizlarkaya

gate

Temple of the
Storm God

Citadel
(Acropolis)

Southern
citadel

Temple VII

Main public thoroughfare

Ceremonial route

UPPER CITY

SARIKALE

Temple VI

Lion
Gateway

King's
Gateway

YENICEKALE

Temple II

Temple IV

Temple V

Temple III

N

Sphinx
Gateway

Hattusa, c. 1200 BC

Present-day town

0   500 yards

0   500 metres

LEFT: The ruins identifed by archaeologist Hugo Winckler as the Hittite capital of Hattusa.

BELOW: The Lion Gate guards one of the entrances to the city.

Fortunately, in 1834 the French architect and archaeologist Charles Texier was conducting an expedition in the Anatolian region of Turkey. Around 100 miles (160km) east of the modern Turkish capital Ankara, he unearthed the monumental ruins of what had quite obviously been a vast city at Boghaskoy (Bogazkale), along with some smaller remains of a temple or holy place a mile or so away at Yazılıkaya. Texier died before the full significance of his discovery was known. But following decades of further physical and intellectual spadework, the German archeologist Hugo Winckler was finally and conclusively able to identify the ruins as Hattusa – the previously only speculated upon epicentre of the Hittite Empire.

Archeological evidence points to a settlement at Hattusa as far back as the sixth millennium BC. Traces of carbon also show that the Hittites built their capital on the torched remnants of a previous city; one established in the early Bronze Age but which had been burnt to the ground in around 1700 BC. The same fate was long believed to have eventually befallen the Hittites own metropolis and at the hands of marauders known as the Sea People in about 1190 BC, after which date the Hittites cease to bother contemporary chroniclers. But more recent research suggests that the city had already been partly abandoned by that time and its demise was a less sudden and violent affair. We do know, however, that at various stages in its history Hittite Hattusa was assailed by hostile forces and came close to being destroyed by invading tribes around 1400 BC. After that the city was enlarged, doubling in size, and was rebuilt, with massive new fortifications that extended over 4 miles (8km) and a second protective curtain wall lined with towers was added for good measure. The entrances to the city were decorated with monumental relief sculptures. Such artistic flourishes today supply its partially reconstructed walls with their arresting namesakes, the Lion, Sphinx and Warrior God gates.

At its peak, covering an area of 407 acres (165 hectares), Hattusa was one of the largest capitals of the ancient world. It was comprised of an older 'Lower City', dominated by the royal acropolis, palaces and their most sacred temple to their Weather or Storm God, and a newer 'Upper City' extension that subsequent excavations have revealed was itself equipped with at least twenty-six additional temples.

If religiously observant, the Hittites were also a literate culture, as shown by the discovery at Hattusa, at the end of the nineteenth century, of thousands of clay tablets etched with a unique hieroglyphic script that, although similar to the cuneiform used by the Assyrians, Babylonians and Persians, was entirely unknown until then. Once the script was deciphered, this store of documents supplied scholars with a detailed account of the life and times of the Hittite empire and its relations with arch-rivals such as the Egyptians. What they remain silent on, however, is just how and why Hattusa fell and what became of its formerly so mighty inhabitants.

HATTUSA

LEPTIS MAGNA

LIBYA

32° 38' 13.8" N / 14° 17' 37.4" E

The Phoenicians are famed as exceptional mariners, whose mighty ships, adorned with horses' heads in honour of their sea god Yamm, accomplished epic sea voyages thanks to their advanced knowledge of navigation. Their world was composed of a series of independent city-states lying on a strip of the Mediterranean coast mapped by modern Syria, Lebanon and northern Israel. They have been credited with inventing curved hulled boats, the alphabet, purple dye and possibly glassware, and introducing the domesticated cat into Europe – Phoenician sailors noticed that the felines were efficient rat catchers and duly took them aboard their vessels as pest controllers, carrying them to Italy and beyond. Examples of their wares have been found as far north as Great Britain, and one of the finest cities in the Roman Empire, Leptis Magna, began its life as a Phoenician trading post, Lpqy, in the seventh century BC.

Situated on the Mediterranean shores of north Africa, with Malta and Italy just a short distance across the sea, and lying at the mouth of the Wadi Lebda in present-day Libya, what appealed to the Phoenicians about the location of this particular outpost was the potential promise of access to the inland caravan routes. The settlement, which was centred around a harbour on the Wadi Lebda, seemingly grew into a substantial Phoenician colony and later fell within the dominions of the Carthaginian Empire. But whatever commercial or even architectural achievements it mustered then – and the latter were largely submerged without trace below layer upon layer of later developments – pales into insignificance when placed against its subsequent Roman incarnation.

From the reign of the first Roman Emperor, Augustus, Leptis lay within the Roman province of Africa Proconsularis and, if still a trading port, was by then becoming better known for its agriculture

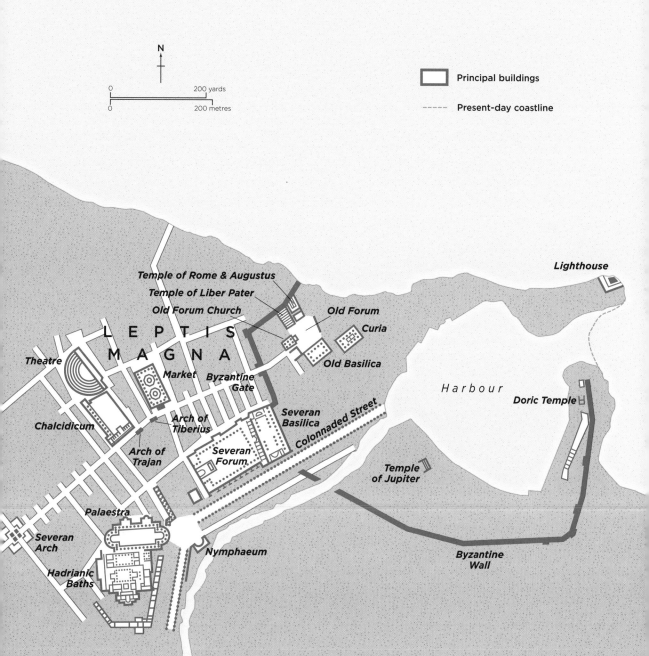

Mediterranean Sea

N

0   200 yards
0   200 metres

☐ Principal buildings

----- Present-day coastline

Lighthouse

Temple of Rome & Augustus
Temple of Liber Pater
Old Forum Church
Old Forum
Curia

L E P T I S
M A G N A

Old Basilica

Theatre

Market   **Byzantine**
Gate

Harbour

Doric Temple

Chalcidicum

Severan
Basilica

Arch of
Tiberius

Colonnaded Street

Arch of
Trajan

Severan
Forum

Temple
of Jupiter

Palaestra

Severan
Arch

Nymphaeum

Byzantine
Wall

Hadrianic
Baths

and especially the cultivation of olive oil, which from this period was to intensify dramatically. While much of the terrain is semidesert, the city was gifted with a hinterland of rich fertile soil that seemed almost peculiarly well suited to olive tree growth, and also a series of wadis that helped irrigate crops in the absence of rainfall. Leptis was to become astonishingly wealthy on the back of olive oil. This product lubricated the Roman world, supplying Emperor and slave alike with the staple source of fat in their diets, the means to clean themselves via olive-oil based soaps and the chance to illuminate the dark as a fuel for lighting. Gallons upon gallons were exported to every corner of the Empire from Leptis's harbour.

Leptis in turn developed into one of the most Romanized cities of north Africa as the wealthy elite competed with each other to erect public buildings – the requisite temples, a forum, theatre, an aqueduct and public baths, amphitheatre, a circus for chariot races, etc., – to give their home city all the comforts of the imperial capital.

The city's status rose considerably, though, after one of its sons, Lucius Septimius Severus seized the Imperial throne in AD 193, becoming, in the opinion of leading historians of the site, 'the first truly provincial Emperor'. Severus was not to forget his roots, granting his birthplace the prestige of counting itself as a full Roman city, an honour that came with considerable attendant tax breaks, and bankrolling a major building programme to transform it into a metropolis fit for an emperor.

Under these schemes, which were only completed after Severus's death and during the reign of his son and successor Caracalla, Leptis's

BELOW: The theatre at Leptis Magna combines elements of both Greek and Roman theatres.

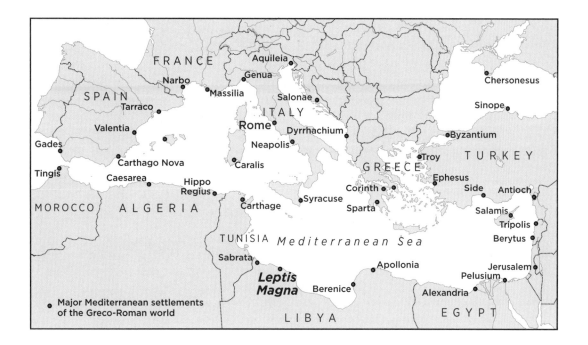

Map labels: FRANCE · Aquileia · Genua · Narbo · Massilia · SPAIN · Tarraco · Salonae · ITALY · Rome · Chersonesus · Sinope · Valentia · Neapolis · Dyrrhachium · Byzantium · Gades · Caralis · Troy · TURKEY · Tingis · Carthago Nova · GREECE · Ephesus · Caesarea · Hippo Regius · Corinth · Side · Antioch · MOROCCO · ALGERIA · Carthage · Syracuse · Sparta · Salamis · Tripolis · Berytus · TUNISIA · Mediterranean Sea · Sabrata · Apollonia · Jerusalem · Pelusium · Leptis Magna · Berenice · Alexandria · EGYPT · Major Mediterranean settlements of the Greco-Roman world · LIBYA

ABOVE: Leptis Magna's place amongst other major settlements in the Greco-Roman world.

NEXT PAGE: The arch of the Roman Emperor Septimius Severus.

harbour was made over with a marble colonnaded avenue for a slipway. The city gained a massive new forum and basilica, and a triumphal arch embellished with sculptural depictions of the Severus clan at the centre of its main crossroads. Predictably the pace of redevelopment slackened after the passing of the Severus dynasty, and what stood already was then subjected to a run of earthquakes in the AD 360s along with raids by nomadic peoples in the same period. The city rallied a little under East Roman or Byzantine command in the fifth century but was by then a shrunken husk of its former self with its harbour inconveniently on the verge of silting up. By the time the Arabs conquered the region in about AD 643, the city appears already to have been abandoned. The same shifting sands that served as pathways for the caravans that had led the Phoenicians here in the first place, soon enough engulfed Leptis's ruins.

The city slumbered on until the Victorian era, its peace interrupted only by intermittent bouts of petty thieving, with the likes of Claude Lemaire, a French consul in Tripoli in the seventeenth century, shipping chunks of purloined Leptis marble back to Paris where it was most probably incorporated into the altar of the church of St Germain des Prés. But the full extent of its architectural treasures was only unearthed in the 1960s, when a series of digs were undertaken. After which time, Libya's political situation and the dictatorial regime of Muammar Gaddafi removed it from the view of the world at large. If perhaps now easier to reach since Gaddafi's death in 2011, at the time of writing most western governments advise against travel to Libya, citing the potential risk of terrorism following the Daesh attack on Tripoli in 2018.

XANADU

MONGOLIA/CHINA

42° 21' 28.9" N / 116° 11' 06.3" E

Deriving from an old children's game, incidentally first called Russian Scandal, the phrase 'Chinese whispers' is normally used to describe the process where a story (or rumorous gossip) ends up becoming more and more distorted as it is passed from person to person. With each retelling the tale is subtly, or not so subtly, altered until it ends up bearing almost no resemblance to the original report. And in many respects the story of Xanadu, or what most of us think we know about this one-time capital of Mongol-ruled China, feels like an extended game of Chinese whispers, with unreliable accounts, and accounts of unreliable accounts, pilling up over the centuries since its creation.

If its name usually brings anything immediately to mind it is most probably Samuel Taylor Coleridge's famous poem 'Kubla Khan' which begins:

> In Xanadu did Kubla Khan
> A stately pleasure-dome decree:
> Where Alph, the sacred river, ran
> Through caverns measureless to man
> Down to a sunless sea.
> So twice five miles of fertile ground
> With walls and towers were girdled round;
> And there were gardens bright with sinuous rills,
> Where blossomed many an incense-bearing tree;
> And here were forests ancient as the hills,
> Enfolding sunny spots of greenery.

If this poem is justly one of the most famous in the English language, the story of its composition in his native Devon, supplied in a preface

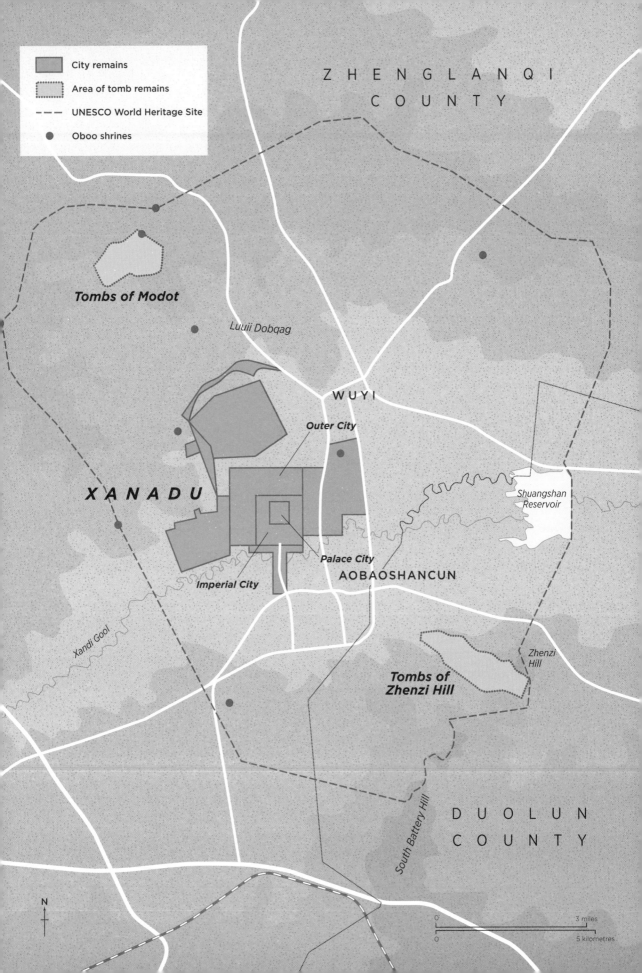

City remains

Area of tomb remains

UNESCO World Heritage Site

Oboo shrines

Z H E N G L A N Q I
C O U N T Y

Tombs of Modot

Luuii Dobqag

W U Y I

Outer City

X A N A D U

Imperial City

Palace City

AOBAOSHANCUN

Xandi Gool

Shuangshan
Reservoir

*Zhenzi
Hill*

**Tombs of
Zhenzi Hill**

South Battery Hill

D U O L U N
C O U N T Y

N

0   3 miles

0   5 kilometres

by Coleridge himself, is almost as well known. The poem, or so he claimed, came to him in a dream during an 'anodyne' (i.e., laudanum-induced) stupor. Waking after about three hours of vision-filled dozing, the poet seized a pen and started furiously writing down the 300-odd lines of verse that had supposedly sprung miraculously fully formed in his head. Unfortunately, he only got as far as the first three stanza before a 'person on business from Porlock' interrupted him. Having been detained for an hour by this factotum, Coleridge returned to his desk eager to commit the rest of the poem to paper only to find he was unable to recall any more of it. Which in the end, might have been for the best, for, not only was he able to spin a memorable yarn about forgetting most of it, but the poem's brevity made it easier to commit to memory and probably didn't harm its long-term prospects in terms of becoming a popular and easy-to-recite classic of literature.

As it happens, prior to drifting off into drug-fuelled sleep, the opium-addicted Coleridge had been engrossed in a seventeenth-century travel book by Samuel Purchas. It was a volume filled with wild accounts of voyages to far-flung and exotic lands left by wide-eyed explorers of yore and scurvy-ridden mariners, of the mostly ancient and albatross-dodging variety. Among them was something taken from Marco Polo's reminisces of his spell in Xanadu, and that appears, somewhat conveniently for all concerned, to have caught Coleridge's eye shortly before he nodded off: 'In Xandu did Cublai Can build a stately Pallace', runs the opening part of this particular Polo passage ....

Marco Polo was accused, until recently, of making it no further than the Bosphorus and was held, in any case, to be an inveterate liar on the basis of some of the more outlandish descriptions of places, people and animals, contained in *Travels of Marco Polo*, the book that has come down to us. But the thirteenth-century Venetian trader and explorer is less readily dismissed as a medieval fantasist these days. A good deal of evidence seems to suggest that he genuinely did reach China, probably first travelling there with his father and uncle in 1271, and most likely did spend a number of years in the service of the court of Kubla Khan in Xanadu. But his memoirs, such as they are, were composed in prison and dictated to his cellmate Rustichello of Pisa. A prolific author of chivalric romances, Rustichello was a man who knew how to spin a tale and what tickled the public's fancy. In Polo he had a shameless braggart for a fellow lag, with twenty-four years' worth of Oriental wanderings to get off his chest and nothing much else pressing to do behind bars.

The Pisan scribe saw no reason, far from it, to rein in some of the old man's more questionable assertions and stitched the thing together with whatever additional flourishes appeared necessary to keep it all rolling along. In time others too would pirate the text, mistranslate what originally appeared in courtly Old French, add and subtract as

ABOVE: The palace of Kubla Khan, from *The Travels of Marco Polo*.

they saw fit, and generally leave a plethora of different versions of the Travels floating around for us to make the best of. For Rustichello, a lot of what Polo said in the first place, even in the calmest of moments, and what he swore, hand on heart, to have seen with own eyes, was difficult enough to believe. And not a little of it concerned his time in Xanadu in the court of an empire where, to the initial astonishment of this seasoned Venetian trader, they used paper money.

This novel form of currency was an innovation of Kubla Khan, grandson of Genghis Khan. A formerly nomadic people, esteemed for their prowess with horses and feared for their pitiless cruelty as warriors, the Mongols under Genghis Khan and his heirs forged a surprisingly tolerant and cosmopolitan empire that at its peak was the largest the world has ever known and that covered nearly all of present-day Eurasia. (Paper cash was not a bad way then, and indeed now, to unify a disparate band of peoples, spread far and wide, and to keep a firm grip on the monetary supply into the bargain.) Kubla Khan ascended to the throne in 1260 at Xanadu, the new city he'd had built a couple of years earlier on the plains of the Jinlianchuan Prairie to the north of the Shandian river in northern China. The city served as his first Imperial capital, although it would later be relegated to a summer royal court. But this was hardly a seasonal Dacha. The city was a metropolis that welcomed emissaries and merchants from across the globe. It was laid out over 96 square miles (25,000 hectares) and composed of three concentric sections, a central Imperial Palace, then the main Imperial City and finally a defensive Outer City. Beyond them, there was a further ring of suburbs that were zoned, to use the contemporary phrase, for military and commercial purposes, with barracks, markets for livestock and other goods, shops, taverns, inns and workshops, along with residential quarters for workmen and traders not permitted to live inside the city itself.

The design and construction of Xanadu was overseen by one of Khan's most trusted Chinese advisors, Liu Bingzhdong. The city was positioned to be in harmony with the nearby river and mountain and offered an unparalleled fusion of Han Chinese and Mongolian elements, boasting, alongside the plentiful areas of open space, gardens and water features, the hunting grounds yearned for by the restless ex-nomads, and ramps called mandaos that allowed the horse and carriage-borne to enter the main palace compound without dismounting. Inside its walls were temples, government offices, pavilions and halls, the grandest of which, and the largest building in the Imperial Palace, was the Muqinq Hall. But it was the Da'an Pavilion that became Xanadu's signature structure – a pavilion of

BELOW: Reliefs and a statue of Kubla Khan in Xanadu.

such stately proportions, that centuries after its destruction it continued to enthrall, if admittedly, in the retrospective, not to say romantic, abstract.

Mongolian rule would end in the fourteenth century, and with it, Xanadu. The succeeding Ming dynasty did not especially care for a city already on the slide and closely associated with Genghis Khan, an enlightened despot whose descendants had by then departed for the steppes. Its ruins would later be scavenged for stone to build houses by the neighbouring town of Dolon Nor and most of the rest of what was left subsumed by encroaching grasslands.

It was only in the 1990s that serious archeological excavations were begun, and in 2011, the site of this major lost city was finally opened to the public, in the process giving visitors the ability to connect with a place that had for so long been the subject of such outlandish speculation, not to say, unfettered invention. The ruins are a wonder. And a museum where hundreds of artefacts are displayed, carefully removed after centuries below ground, gives a sense of what has been lost. But arguably it still takes a slight leap of the imagination to picture what Xanadu must have been like in its prime.

BELOW: The site of Xanadu was made a UNESCO World Heritage site in 2012.

CIUDAD PERDIDA

COLOMBIA

11° 02' 15.3" N / 73° 55' 30.1" W

The Spanish name Ciudad Perdida roughly translates as 'Lost City'. And certainly, to the vast majority of Spanish-speaking Colombians and the wider world, it remained that way until the mid-1970s. It was only then that news of the discovery of ruins high up in the Sierra Mountains of Colombia, which were older and stranger than Peru's storied Inca citadel Machu Picchu, reached the general public. The city had, in fact, been located just a couple of years earlier by a gang of unscrupulous guagüeros, or tomb-raiding treasure seekers. Due to the nefarious nature of their line of work they somewhat unsurprisingly tried to keep its existence to themselves. But if there's one thing unscrupulous guagüeros can't really be trusted with, aside from artefacts of historical interest and financial/sentimental value, it's keeping secrets about their cannier discoveries.* Soon enough rumours spread from one loose-tongued guagüero to another and finally the story reached the ears of an archeologist or two, who notified the authorities fearing the site would be stripped of everything of worth. As it turned out, Spanish conquistadors had beaten the guagüeros to it, having cleared the place of every scrap of precious metal back in 1578, after which time Ciudad Perdida settled into the obscurity that it was only finally to emerge from four centuries later.

Nevertheless, in all that time it was far from lost to one particular group: the indigenous Kogi (or Kogui in some spellings) people, who have lived for generations in the vicinity of the place they know as Teyuna and count themselves as the descendants of the Tayronas who established it.

---

* Without wishing to generalize, for no doubt there are unscrupulous guagüeros who out of self-interest if nothing else have learned to keep their counsel, but in this field of endeavour bragging about finding treasure is almost as sweet as finding it.

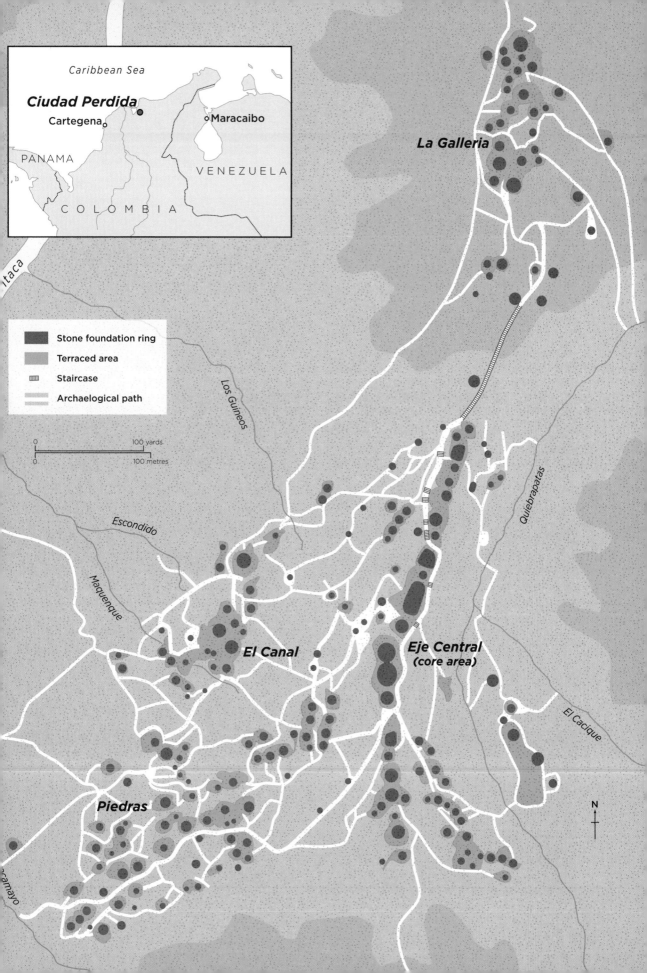

Caribbean Sea

Ciudad Perdida

Cartegena

PANAMA

Maracaibo

VENEZUELA

COLOMBIA

Itaca

La Galleria

Stone foundation ring

Terraced area

Staircase

Archaelogical path

Los Guineos

0   100 yards
0   100 metres

Escondido

Maquenque

El Canal

Eje Central
(core area)

Quiebrapatas

El Cacique

Piedras

N

aramayo

It was the Tayronas' fate ultimately not to survive the arrival of the Europeans in the fifteenth century, wiped out as they were by conquistadors' swords and guns and the diseases they brought with them from the Old World. Before that, however, this largely peaceable race, who fished, farmed and traded goods with other tribes along the Caribbean coast and in the foothills of the Sierra Nevada de Santa Marta range, had already retreated up into the mountains in response to incursions by the no less hostile Caribs from the islands out at sea. Their eventual stronghold, Teyuna, which even to reach today still involves a four-day uphill trek from the coast through the dense jungle of the Buritaca river valley and the scaling of 1,263 raked stone steps, was built in around AD 800 – some 650 years before Machu Picchu in Peru. The original city covered a vast area, of which only around 10 per cent has so far been excavated.

The whole settlement was configured around a quite unparalleled architectural arrangement of circular stone terraces and plazas that cascade down the mountain side. This layering, if unusual but highly inventive, is believed to have served at least two immensely practical purposes. First, this terrace system offered shelter from the rains, and in turn the layers acted as run-off drains that protected the city itself from being washed away by waters rushing down to the river below. Secondly, sections of each terrace layer were likely composted and used to grow crops, with root vegetables, lima beans and cocoa that needed less light planted at lower levels and maize and cotton higher up where they might get more sun, in a scheme of pyramid farming, if you will. Botanists who have examined the flora around Teyuna maintain that it shows marked signs of human cultivation. Its range of plants are richer and quite different from jungle that's never been inhabited elsewhere, and the area's unkempt foliage is closer to a long-gone-to-seed market garden than the untamed wilderness it initially might appear to be.

Of course, the Kogi, whose village settlements surround the remnants of the city, continue to tend the land in age-old ways. These ways have hardly changed since the time of the Tayronas and cohere with their deep-held spiritual belief that the Earth is an organic living being. In striving to exist in complete equilibrium with the environment themselves, the Kogi, who uniformly wear pure, untreated white cotton robes and keep their jet-black hair long, have grave doubts about the rest of mankind. They refer to outsiders, pointedly, as merely 'the children who do not know how to take care of the world'.

For the best part of half a millennium, the Kogi, having used passive resistance to successfully evade the attentions of Spanish conquistadors and Jesuit missionaries alike, enjoyed only a passing relationship with those beyond their ancestral lands. The jungle served as an effective barrier, mostly sequestering them from those below it. Even after the lost city on their doorstep was reported found, those willing to risk

ABOVE: A Kogi village settlement
outside the remnants of the city.

PREVIOUS PAGE: A panoramic
view of the spectacular terraces
of Ciudad Perdida.

the journey were few. By the 1970s, the area's relative seclusion had also come to the attention of those involved in Colombia's booming cocaine trade, with drug lords and their armed gangs operating with impunity away from prying eyes amid the thickets of vines. As recently as 2003 a group of eight tourists and their guide were kidnapped on their way to Ciudad Perdida and held for ransom by one such outfit. But Colombia has become much safer in the last decade and a half and, with government troops policing the region with far greater vigilance than ever before, more tourists have been encouraged to find the lost city. Between 2007 and 2011, the numbers of visitors a year quadrupled from 2,000 to 8,000. While rising far less rapidly since then, the figures have continued to nudge up, little by little, each year to the immense dismay of the Kogi who feel a landscape they view as sacred is being desecrated. Not unreasonably, they fear for the loss of their culture, and the peaceful mode of being that has sustained them virtually unchanged for centuries up to this point.

MAHABALIPURAM

INDIA

12° 36′ 59.4″ N / 80° 11′ 57.2″ E

The tsunami that broke on 26 December 2004 (Boxing Day), is thought to be the deadliest on record. It was triggered by a colossal earthquake on the northern tip of Sumatra. The quake shook for a full ten minutes, causing the earth to vibrate by as much as a centimetre (½in) and displaced enough water in the Indian Ocean to send waves of up to 30m (100ft) high crashing in across Indonesia. Within two hours, the tsunami had reached Sri Lanka, India and Thailand and its effects were to be felt in east Africa and even as far away as North America and Antarctica. More than 230,000 people died across fourteen countries. In the south Indian coastal region of Tamil Nadu at least 1,500 were killed and waves battered one of its most famous landmarks, the Dravidian Temple at Mahabalipuram on the shores of the Bay of Bengal.

However, once the sea had receded, its ferocious scour was shown to have given the temple the equivalent of a brisk deep-clean, removing ages of accumulated grit from reliefs on the building. It also left exposed, for the first time in centuries, granite sculptures previously buried far beneath layers of shoreline sand. A fine lion, parts of an elephant and the image of a stallion reared in flight now emerged blinking into the sunlight. Their reappearance seemed to add force to an ancient myth about Mahabalipuram, that during the period of the Pallava dynasty, who dominated life in this quarter of India between the fourth and ninth century, it was an important maritime centre.

The legend, first chronicled in 1798 by a visiting Englishman called John Goldingham, and much repeated in subsequent accounts of the area, maintained that this coastal outpost was known to mariners of antiquity as the home of the Seven Pagodas. Brahmins, who Goldingham claimed to have spoken with, stated that their ancestors

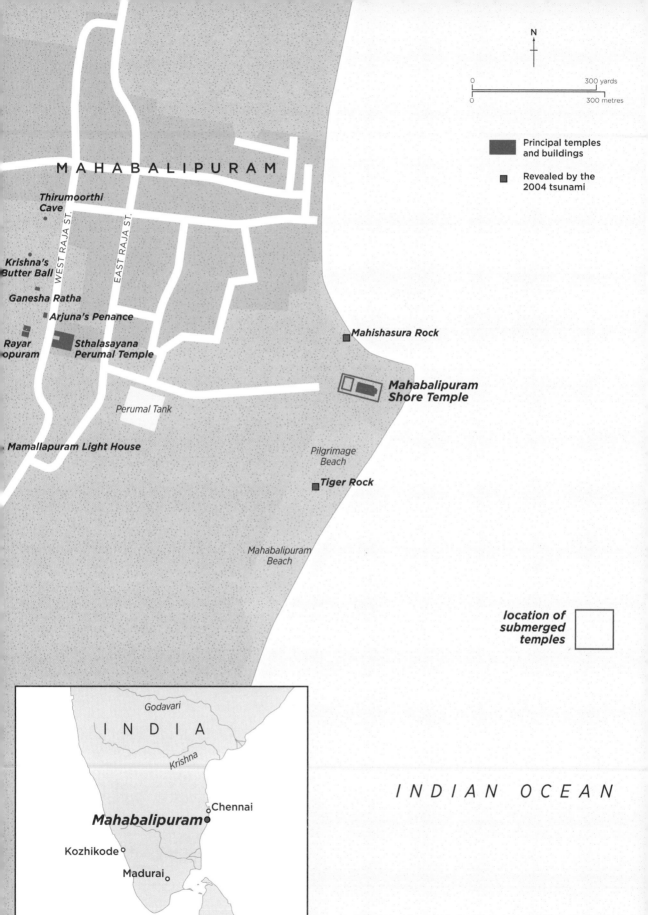

N

0   300 yards
0   300 metres

■ Principal temples and buildings

■ Revealed by the 2004 tsunami

MAHABALIPURAM

Thirumoorthi Cave

WEST RAJA ST.

EAST RAJA ST.

Krishna's Butter Ball

Ganesha Ratha

Arjuna's Penance

Rayar opuram

Sthalasayana Perumal Temple

■ *Mahishasura Rock*

Mahabalipuram Shore Temple

Perumal Tank

Mamallapuram Light House

Pilgrimage Beach

■ *Tiger Rock*

Mahabalipuram Beach

location of submerged temples

Godavari

INDIA

Krishna

Mahabalipuram

o Chennai

Kozhikode o

Madurai o

INDIAN OCEAN

remembered the gilt tops of these supposedly lost temples poking out of the sand. And the original purpose of these structures, aside from religious devotion, was seemingly to help guide vessels to the shore. More mythically, their destruction had been ordained by an angry god who took exception to their beauty and cast down all but one of the seven temples and the port city they allegedly served.

Whatever the truth of these stories, archeologists have pointed out that the main shore temple at Mahabalipuram was built on bedrock, while any near peers were most likely constructed on much weaker sand and thereby faced the whims of the ocean. But investigations into the survival of these curious monuments, experts believe, might well help to preserve other relics threatened by the sea.

ABOVE: Rock carvings unearthed following the 2004 tsunami.

RIGHT: The Shore Temple at Mahabalipuram.

PALENQUE

MEXICO

17° 29' 02.9" N / 92° 02' 45.9" W

It was all supposed to be over on 21 December 2012. Or so those who travelled to Palenque, the ancient Mayan city at Chiapas, Mexico, to see out that year's solstice seemed to believe. Many of them quite fervently so – the solidity of their faith that the world was going to end there and then, underlined by the purchase of one-way tickets. But in the end, the ending didn't come. Clocks, even those set to observe the Long Count, the Mayan calendar whose final hours of its 5,200-year cycle were said to be approaching, blithely ticked on. The sun, confoundingly, rose once more, and sighs of relief (or disappointment) echoed around Palenque as the light glanced off its mighty pyramid and another day dawned in utter defiance of the worse predictions.

Still, endings come in many different forms as Palenque perhaps could have told them. There it was, one of the most important cities in the Classic Period of Maya civilization (*c.* AD 250–900), a regal centre of commerce, art, religious observance and bloody human sacrifice. Palenque's store of plazas, temples, tombs, aqueducts and stelae (commemorative stone monuments etched with hieroglyphic inscriptions) was added to by a succession of kings, all following the bold example set by, perhaps its great builder monarch, Pakal the Great in the sixth century. Yet come *c.* AD 950 it was done; or undone more accurately, by tribal warfare, failing agriculture and population decline. Palenque, like all the other central Mayan cities (Tikal, Copán and Yaxchilán), was deserted and abandoned for a fresh start on the north Yucatan coastal plains; a place where the Long Count calendar, an invention of those former Mayan metropolises, fell into disuse as well.

TOP: A stucco motif of Pakal the Great on display at the Archaeological Museum of Palenque.

BOTTOM: The Temple of the Inscriptions at Palenque, which also houses the tomb of Pakal the Great.

The temples and palaces at Palenque meanwhile were absorbed by the surrounding jungle; the vegetation helping to preserve its painted stonework and dissuade looters from absconding with its ornamental artworks. This lost city would not be found again until the sixteenth century, when a Spanish priest Father Pedro Lorenzo de la Nada, stumbled upon it with the help of a native guide during an exploration of the area. Its full exhumation would nevertheless have to wait another four hundred years, with one of the major breakthroughs coming with the discovery of Pakal the Great's tomb by the Mexican archaeologist Alberto Ruz Lhuillier in 1952.

RIGHT: The palace of Palenque in 1956.

FOLLOWING PAGE: The surrounding jungle helped to preserve the ruins of Palenque.

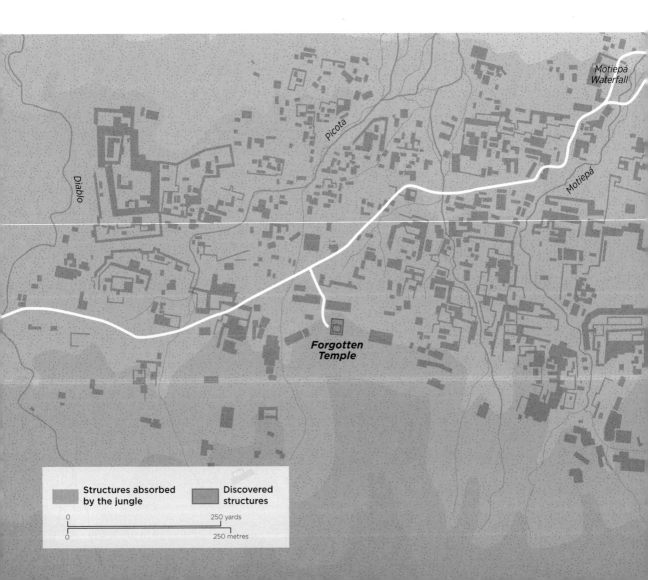

Diablo

Picota

Motiepá Waterfall

Motiepá

Forgotten Temple

Structures absorbed by the jungle

Discovered structures

0   250 yards

0   250 metres

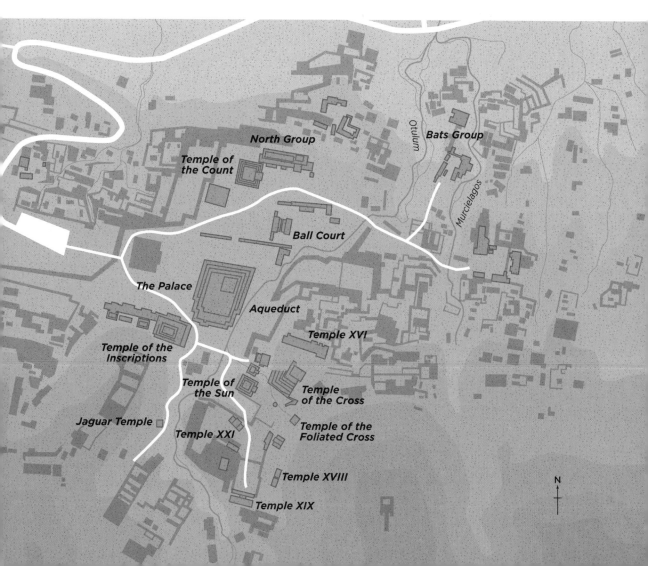

Temple of
the Count

North Group

Otulum

Bats Group

Murcielagos

Ball Court

The Palace

Aqueduct

Temple XVI

Temple of the
Inscriptions

Temple of
the Sun

Temple
of the Cross

Jaguar Temple

Temple XXI

Temple of the
Foliated Cross

Temple XVIII

Temple XIX

N

HELIKE

GREECE

38° 13' 02.7" N / 22° 08' 01.5" E

Of all the Olympians of Ancient Greece, and to be honest they were a pretty rum bunch of Gods – petty, devious, incestuous, licentious, murderous and worse – Poseidon was the one you were probably best off not annoying, as the story of his feud with Odysseus in Homer's *The Odyssey* makes more than plain. God of the sea but also creator of the horse, Poseidon is invariably described as ill-humoured and angry and endlessly to be found fuming about the oceans in a chariot with a trident in hand. This weapon was also deployed to strike the ground and trigger earthquakes whenever the (bad) mood caught him. In the choice words of one chronicler of the Greek myths, Poseidon's wrath is said to have been 'incalculable' while even his eyebrows were 'massive and threatening'. But then many of us might have 'anger issues', to use the modern therapy speak, if we'd been eaten at birth by our own fathers.

The good people of Helike, for a time an important city in the northern part of the Peloponnese peninsula, had at least shown Poseidon some love. They had nominated him as their city's protector and deity of choice, stuck him on their coins, praised him in their temples and erected a great statue of his likeness in bronze, wild beard, threatening eyebrows, trident, and all. But somehow there was a problem with the statue.

The stories vary: in some accounts, the God of the sea wanted them to lend it to some visiting Ionians; in other versions of the tale he was simply unhappy with how it looked. Whatever it was, the statue appears to have earned Helike the wrath of Poseidon and he decided to punish the city by destroying it over a single night in the winter of 373 BC.

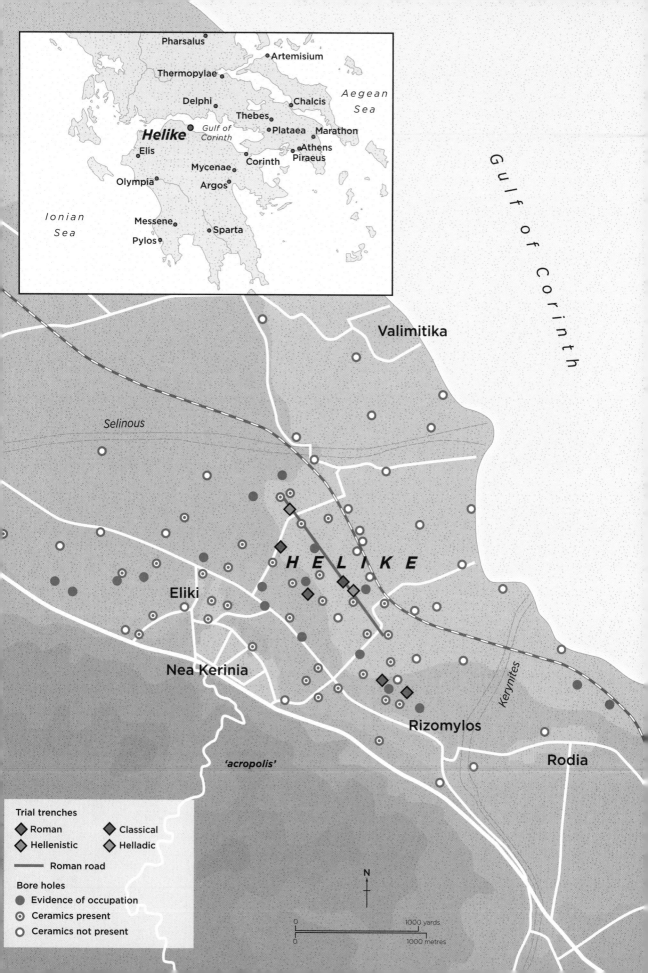

Inset map (top left)

Pharsalus

Artemisium

Thermopylae

Delphi

Chalcis

Thebes

Plataea

Helike

Marathon

Gulf of Corinth

Elis

Athens

Piraeus

Mycenae

Corinth

Olympia

Argos

Ionian Sea

Aegean Sea

Messene

Sparta

Pylos

Main map

Gulf of Corinth

Valimitika

Selinous

H E L I K E

Eliki

Kerynites

Nea Kerinia

Rizomylos

Rodia

'acropolis'

Trial trenches

◆ Roman ◆ Classical

◆ Hellenistic ◆ Helladic

— Roman road

Bore holes

● Evidence of occupation

◉ Ceramics present

○ Ceramics not present

N

0   1000 yards

0   1000 metres

ABOVE: Illustration by Walter Crane. Some ancient stories attributed the loss of Helike to the wrath of the Sea God.

The impending doom, according to legend, was prefigured by the appearance of flaming columns around the city and the flight of all the animals to the mountains in the hours before the massive earthquake hit. As buildings and streets collapsed, a huge tidal wave surged in from the Gulf of Corinth, drowning Helike in an instant and leaving no survivors. For centuries afterwards, the city lay preserved underwater. The head and trident of the statue of Poseidon were, according to the Ancient Greek philosopher Eratosthenes, cursed by local fishermen for causing damage to their nets whenever they sailed over the lost city. Slowly, Helike faded from memory as the saltwater of the sea ate into its ruins, and as Imperial Greece and then Rome passed, its location was forgotten over the centuries. Nevertheless, the story of an ancient city submerged under the sea lingered on, becoming more readily associated with the legend of Atlantis that no one, to date, has been able to find.

It would involve nearly two hundred years of speculation but, finally, in 2001 Helike was rediscovered at Achaea in west Greece. This followed nearly two decades of dedicated research by the Greek archaeologist, Dora Katsonopoulou, who back in 1988 had first suggested that the city might have been located further inland rather than on the coast and ended up beneath a lagoon rather than in the sea at the Gulf of Corinth. The lagoon itself is no more, having silted up over a millennia, and burying Helike under layers of mud as it went. Ongoing excavations are only now peeling back those layers and bringing to light a city lost to both water and dust since antiquity.

BELOW: Excavations of a Hellenistic-era building, possibly used as a dye-works at modern Eliki village, Achaea.

PETRA

JORDAN

30° 19' 44.0" N / 35° 26' 34.0" E

As one historian has observed, of all the gifted peoples of the ancient world from the Babylonians and the Assyrians to the Ancient Greeks, 'the Nabateans are the most unjustly forgotten'. If they are remembered at all today it is largely because of Petra, their majestic fortress city hewn from, and encircled by, the pinkish-red sandstone mountain rock of the Rift Valley. Yet this epicentre of Nabatean life, in what is modern Jordan, was lost to the world for close to a thousand years, its disappearance for so long, naturally enough, only adding to the cultural amnesia surrounding a civilization whose exact beginnings remain as hazy as a desert mirage.

Formerly an entirely nomadic people who appear to have resisted the allure of permanent settlements and agriculture long after near contemporaries started to embrace them, the Nabateans are believed to be Arabs and variously ascribed to hail originally from either Yemen, the east of Bahrain or north west of present-day Saudi Arabia. At some point between the sixth and fourth centuries BC, they are thought to have migrated west to occupy, if still peripatetically, lands to the north west of Arabia, in the region between Syria and Egypt and immortalized in Old Testament scripture as the former home of the Edomites. Seemingly the Nabateans spent the subsequent century or so, continuing to eek out a hardscrabble existence here, leading flocks of sheep and camels across this semi-arid landscape and subsisting on a diet of meat, wild plants and milk laced with honey, and intermittently resorting to brigandry whenever necessity demanded it.

Gradually, however, their wanderings gained a fresh mercantile purpose. From a strategically important base at the junction of the main caravan trails and near the fresh-water springs flowing from the Wadi Musa, the Nabateans began to involve themselves in the

growing trade in aromatics, such as frankincense and myrrh, between North Africa and Southern Arabia and the Mediterranean world. They also turned their arm to transporting bitumen from the Dead Sea through the Sinai desert to Egypt. Within a relative short period, the adaptable Nabateans transformed themselves into canny and very prosperous couriers and merchants, soon gaining a commanding hand in all the major trading routes.

Equally they were to prove skilled architectural engineers and talented agrarians and artisans who produced some of the finest pottery in the ancient world. By the second century BC, they possessed a kingdom whose influence stretched from Syria in the north and Arabia to the south, and the Negev in the west and to Al-Jawf in the east. Their capital at Petra, a metropolitan oasis that flourished thanks to ample supplies of fresh water, hidden within rocky mountains, and surrounded by semi-arid desert, earned a reputation as a pre-eminent emporium of the Middle East; one that was deemed important enough to be honoured by visits from Greek diplomats during the late Hellenic period.

By all accounts, though, Petra's golden age would come between the first century BC and around AD 106 when, following the death of the last Nabatean king, Rabbel II, their dominions were finally subsumed, evidently peaceably, into the Roman Empire and the city remained prosperous enough through the Byzantine era.

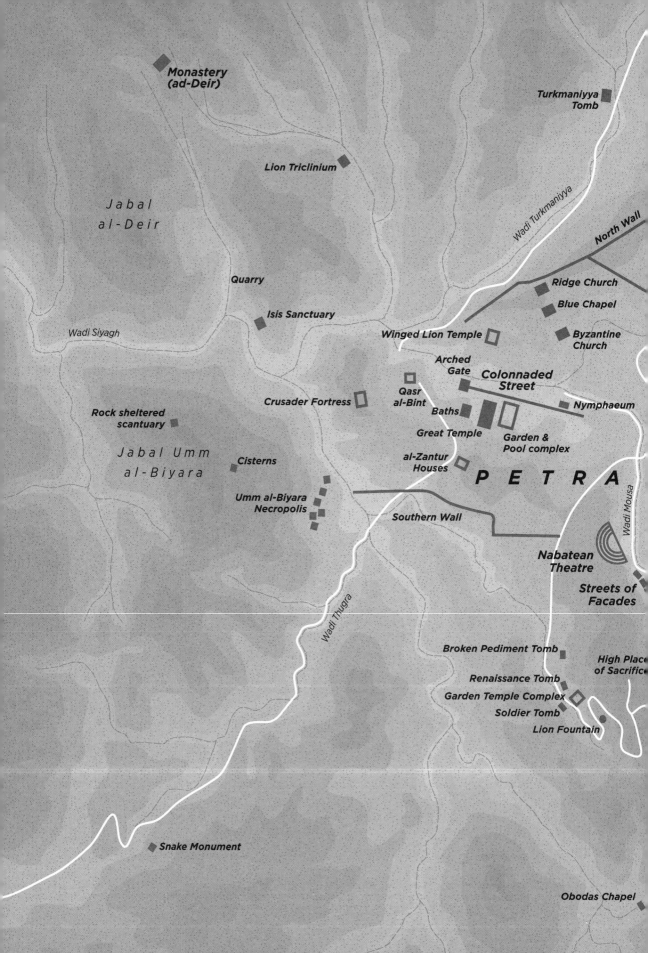

Monastery (ad-Deir)

Turkmaniyya Tomb

Jabal al-Deir

Lion Triclinium

Wadi Turkmaniyya

North Wall

Ridge Church

Blue Chapel

Quarry

Byzantine Church

Isis Sanctuary

Wadi Siyagh

Winged Lion Temple

Arched Gate

Colonnaded Street

Qasr al-Bint

Crusader Fortress

Baths

Nymphaeum

Rock sheltered scantuary

Great Temple

Garden & Pool complex

Jabal Umm al-Biyara

Cisterns

al-Zantur Houses

P E T R A

Umm al-Biyara Necropolis

Southern Wall

Wadi Mousa

Nabatean Theatre

Streets of Facades

Wadi Thugra

Broken Pediment Tomb

High Place of Sacrifice

Renaissance Tomb

Garden Temple Complex

Soldier Tomb

Lion Fountain

Snake Monument

Obodas Chapel

Mughar an-Nasara
Necropolis

Aqueduct

Conway Tower

Wadi Mataha

al-Wu'eira
Crusader Fortress

Sextius Florentinus Tomb

Byzantine Wall

Palace Tomb

Corinthian Tomb

Silk Tomb

Royal Tombs

Urn Tomb

*Jabal
al-Khubth*

al-Khubth
High Place

Unieshu Tomb

Eagle Monument

Tomb of the 17 Graves

W A D I   M U S A

The Siq (al-Siq)

Wadi Mousa

Asiah
Triclinium

Djinn
Blocks

Entrance
Arch

Snake Tomb

**Treasury
(al-Khazneh)**

**Obelisk
Tomb**

*Jabal
al-Qaratya*

N

0   500 yards

0   500 metres

With a main approach along a winding track through a long natural cleft in the mountains known as the Siq, Petra (which means simply 'rock') concealed its glories behind what must have once been a near impenetrable defensive barricade of rose-red cliffs. Once inside, the visitor is immediately confronted by the magnificent spectacle of the elaborately carved stone facade of the al-Khazneh, or Treasury, though this epic building is most likely a royal tomb, and was probably cut out of the rock during the long reign of Aretas (9 BC–AD 40) when the city may also have acquired many of its grandest processional walkways, temples, palaces and private homes. A unique and fascinating agglomeration of eastern decorative and architectural styles, and teeming with Ptolemaic Egyptian details, Petra was largely laid out along familiar classical Greco-Roman lines with a central inhabited area, or polis; a high place, or acropolis; and a necropolis, or outlying ring of tombs for the dead and chambers of remembrance.

But the eventual conquest of the Byzantine Roman states of Syria, Palestine and Lebanon by Islamic forces in AD 636, and the subsequent establishment of Baghdad as the new capital of the Muslim world, seem to have destroyed Petra as a city of significance. Archeological evidence of damage to certain structures suggests it may also have been subjected to an earthquake or some other kind of environmental catastrophe. All but empty by the time Christian crusaders created a fort on the summit of the neighbouring al-Habi mountain, it was left

ABOVE: The winding track of the Siq provided a barricade for the ancient city.

OPPOSITE: The first glimpse of the carved stone facade of the al-Khazneh, or the Treasury.

to a dusty abandonment and ruination thereafter. Any goings on there were to be mutely observed by passing Bedouin tribesmen for the best part of a millennium.

We owe its rediscovery in the opening part of the nineteenth century to Johann Ludwig Burckhardt. The son of a Swiss Colonel in the French Army, Burckhardt was to spend the bulk of his short life, as one chronicler of his deeds has put it, 'exploring the Near East successfully disguised as a Moslem [sic]'. If never formally converting to the religion, he was nevertheless eventually buried in the Muslim cemetery in Cairo as Ibrahim ibn Abdallah, the name he had adopted, along with suitably convincing costumes, for his travels in the region. These were undertaken with dedication, earnest intent and no lack of personal risk, under the auspices of Joseph Banks' Association for Promoting the Discovery of the Interior Parts of Africa. Burckhardt, after schooling himself in Arabic and the Koran, initially travelled to Syria where he joined a camel caravan to Aleppo before embarking on further, and often extremely hazardous, excursions inland to the ancient ruined city of Palmyra and south to Damascus and on to Tripoli, Lebanon and the biblical lands. It was while passing through the rolling hills of Moab (Jordan) that he began to hear talk of a fabled city buried in a heart of mountains in the near distance that he surmised must be the long-lost Petra of dim legend. On the pretext of a making a sacrifice to the Prophet Aaron, whose tomb was in the vicinity, he not only contrived to reach it in 1812 under the watchful gaze of his highly suspicious local guides but also managed to sketch a basic plan of its layout and location.

After a further five years of frenzied travel to Abyssinia (Ethiopia), Sudan, Jedda and Egypt, Burckhardt contracted dysentery and died on 17 October 1817, aged just 33. The journals he kept throughout these voyages, and usually in conditions of immense secrecy to avoid blowing his cover, were published posthumously. But even before these volumes appeared, revealing once and for all his rediscovery of Petra, Burckhardt's news and his plan had been circulating among other Western adventurers in the Near East.

The next Europeans to reach it in 1818, were a party of seasoned and scholarly British seekers of antiquities. Far from travelling incognito, messers, William John Bankes, Thomas Legh, C.L. Irby and J. Mangles and co., arrived primed with Burckhardt's directions and a good supply of horses, servants, guns, provisions and gold coins, along with the support of a cavalcade of Bedouin horsemen and the blessings of local sheikhs. Their two days at the ruins yielded a 10,000-word report on their findings and a plethora of drawings by Bankes that remain an invaluable record of the state of Petra after its centuries of neglect. Although, as it happens, these pictures would languish unpublished in a cabinet at his ancestral pile, Kingston Lacy in Dorset, until 1981.

True Petra-mania would really begin soon after the French archaeologist and explorer Léon de Laborde published an account of his successful 1828 expedition to Petra with Louis Linant de Bellefonds, the future mastermind behind the Suez Canal. *Voyage de l'Arabie Pétrée* first appeared in France in 1830 and in a lavish folio edition boasting some twenty plates of illustrations that were nothing short of a revelation to the general public. Promptly translated into English and produced in a much cheaper, less picture-heavy edition in 1836, the book established Petra as a place of romantic and spiritual

pilgrimage for often biblically inclined Victorian tourists to the Holy Lands from both Britain and America. In the following century, archaeologists would conduct detailed scientific excavations on the site, revealing that there were among 619 rock-cut tombs in the city and even more rock-cut anterooms, and chambers for dwelling and cultural activities. Discoveries are still being made. Even though Petra has had to contend with being in a location troubled by political and religious tensions for many decades now, it remains that endlessly fascinating 'rose-red city half as old as Time'.

BELOW: The Monastery is hidden high in the hills, similar in design to the Treasury, but far bigger.

TIMGAD

ALGERIA

35° 29′ 05.7″ N / 6° 28′ 06.6″ E

The Romans ruled north-east Africa for more than six hundred years. The province in turn supplied the Empire with a ruling imperial dynasty in the form of the Libyan-born conqueror of Scotland, Septimius Severus and his offspring; and no shortage of soldiers, lawyers, senators and thinkers, among them the early Christian theologian Augustine of Hippo. As the historian of Roman Africa Susan Raven has written, 'it was in some ways the most romanized of all Rome's subject territories, and in its turn it influenced the destiny of the Empire'. Whereas Rome established just sixty cities across Gaul, those in a relatively tight 140-square-mile (26,250-hectare) area of its north African dominions numbered over six hundred. What is left of one of them, Timgad, or Thamugadi – a spectre preserved in part by the whims of the gods, who helpfully put it to sleep beneath a blanket of Saharan sand – stands as an extraordinary remnant of a solid provincial Roman settlement.

Lying on the northern slopes of the Aurès mountains, it was laid out from scratch (*ex nihilo*, as the Latin would have it), and with some precision as a fortified military colony for veterans of the Third Augusta Legion by the Emperor Trajan in AD 100. Situated on the southernmost frontier of the Empire, its purposes were as much strategic as pastoral. But just as the Romans would forge roads further southwards into the country, so Timgad expanded beyond the immaculate chessboard of its original city limits, its new suburbs developing with, as Tim Cornell and John Mathews' *Atlas of the Roman World* puts it, a 'cheerful unconcern for the design of military planners'. Beyond the ramparts, major new public buildings alongside plush residences would mushroom: temples, markets, squares, a

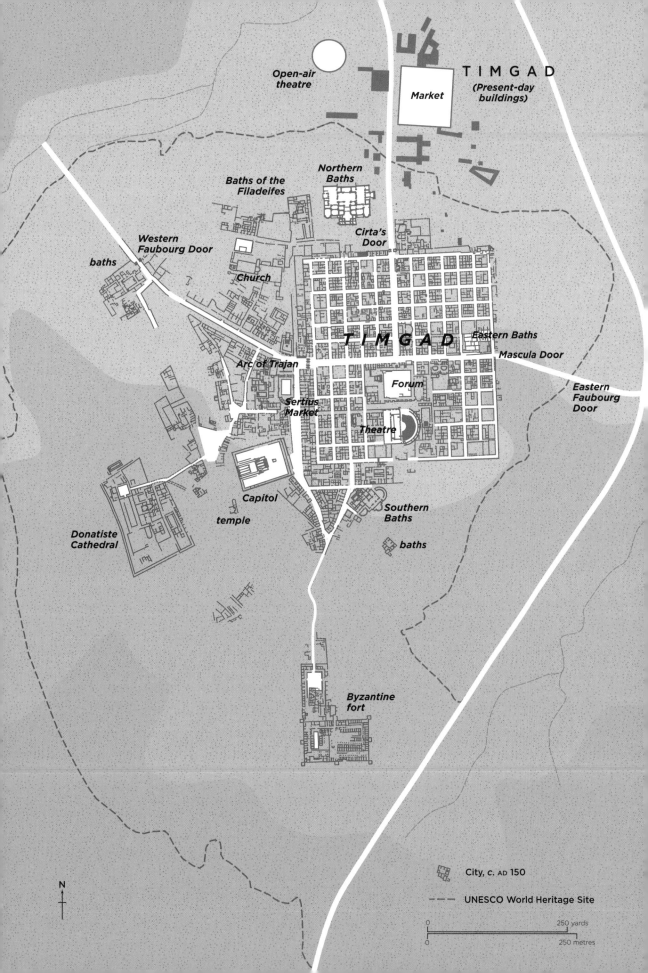

Open-air
theatre

Market

TIMGAD
(Present-day
buildings)

Northern
Baths

Baths of the
Filadeifes

Cirta's
Door

Western
Faubourg Door

baths

Church

Eastern Baths

T I M G A D

Mascula Door

Arc of Trajan

Forum

Eastern
Faubourg
Door

Sertius
Market

Theatre

Capitol

Southern
Baths

temple

baths

Donatiste
Cathedral

Byzantine
fort

N

City, c. AD 150

- - - UNESCO World Heritage Site

0   250 yards
0   250 metres

theatre, an arch in honour of Trajan, and, most impressively, a library and an astonishing fourteen bathhouses. The profusion of the latter is a testament to the popularity of this Roman import in Africa, where they proved as important a factor in the life of the continent's imperial cities as a forum or the curia. (At Timgad, the paving outside the forum bears the scratched inscription: 'Hunting, bathing, gaming, laughing, that's living', implying that its denizens were a far from stuffy bunch.)

By the fourth century, the city also had many churches and a Donatist basilica but in the centuries to come it would be overwhelmed by assaults from the indigenous tribes of the Aurès Mountains and suffer a fatal drubbing by Arab invaders. It was completely uninhabited by the seventh century with the city slowly disappearing beneath the sands over time. It would wait the best part of a thousand years to be reclaimed by the French architect and archeologist, Albert Ballu whose excavations in 1881 brought parts of the city to the surface once more.

RIGHT: Postcard of the ruins at Timgad, *c.* 1910, excavated a few decades earlier.

BELOW: The grid design of the ancient city was typical of Roman design.

RUINES ROMAINES de TIMGAD. — *Voie du Decumanus Maximus* — Collections ND Phot

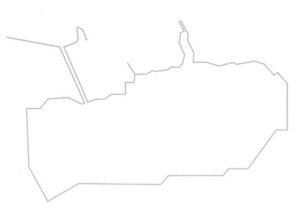

ALEXANDRIA

EGYPT

31° 12′ 01.8″ N / 29° 53′ 41.0″ E

To be bright is to be brainy, and knowledge is similarly associated with enlightenment; to be dull is the opposite of entertaining and dimness a pejorative applied to the intellectually less able. Even the term 'argue', for an exchange of opinions or ideas (or, on occasions, insults), comes from the Ancient Greek *argos*, 'to shine white', that also gives us argent for the precious metal silver and consequently Argentina, 'the land of silver'. In antiquity though, one city was doubly blessed with brightness in every sense of the word. For Alexandria possessed not only its famous lighthouse at Pharos, one of the seven wonders of the ancient world, but also the Library, which was the greatest repository of all the known works of literature, science, mathematics and philosophy. This unparalleled collection of the written word, including works by Plato and Aristotle, was put at the disposal of an elite circle of scholars who formed a seat of learning known as the Museum; named after the muses, the nine inspirational goddesses of the arts and science in Greek mythology.

Centuries before all this, though, Alexandria had been humble Rhakotis, an insignificant little fishing village on the far western tip of the Nile delta. Situated between Lake Mariout and the Mediterranean Sea on the northeastern shores of Egypt, its proximity to Greece, via a direct sea voyage from Rhodes on the corner of the Aegean, would ensure its future prosperity. After conquering Egypt in 332–331 BC, Alexander the Great had himself crowned as pharaoh at Memphis, the nation's ancient capital south of Giza at the mouth of the Nile. But looking to establish another base in Egypt more closely aligned geographically to the rest of his dominions, he chose Rhakotis for the site of a new city that would bear his name. Alexandria most probably became Alexander's final resting place, too, though the precise location of his tomb and the whereabouts of any remains (reputedly initially preserved in honey and then stored in a golden casket) continues to be disputed. In the most widely accepted version of events, his funeral cortege, bound for Macedonia from Babylon, was diverted to Egypt under the wiles of Ptolemy I Soter.

One of Alexander's leading Macedonian generals but also the Egyptian governor, Ptolemy I Soter was to take advantage of the power vacuum left in the region by the childless great leader's death and the almost immediate unravelling of his empire. Possession of Alexander's earthly remains, however deviously obtained, was certainly one way of signally a kind of royal seal of approval of a succession. And in 306 BC, Ptolemy finally obtained the crown of Egypt and all its neighbouring territories. Still, however ill-gotten that gain, the dynasty that Ptolemy inaugurated would rule Egypt for three hundred years. It ushered in an almost unprecedented epoch of relative political and cultural stability, and immense patronage of the arts and sciences. Its finale would come with the suicide in 30 BC of the last Ptolemic ruler, Cleopatra VII Philopator.

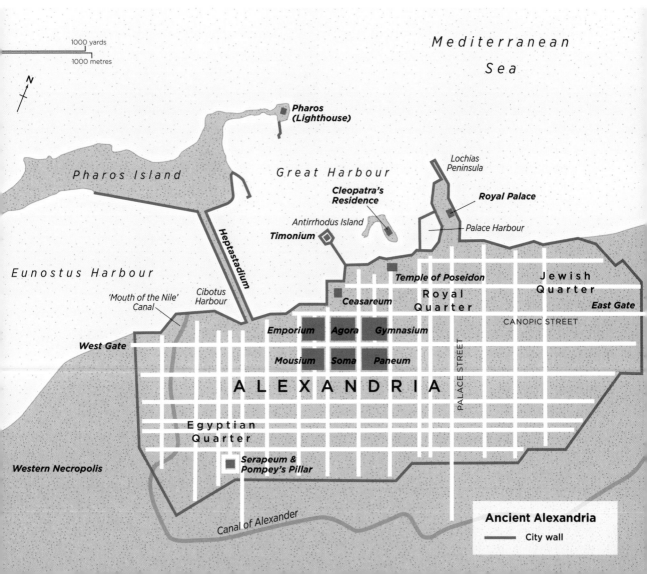

Among the most momentous of Ptolemy's early decisions, however, was to move the Egyptian court (and seemingly Alexander's tomb with it) from Memphis to Alexandria in 313 BC. If, unfortunately, ultimately causing the former to wane into irrelevance, it resulted in the latter growing, with the continuing support of his heirs, into one of the greatest cities in the ancient Hellenic world. And with its location – facing out into the Mediterranean – and its design – planned around an orderly, classical grid layout – Alexandria was a deliberately, self-consciously Greek city in Egypt, with the Royal Necropolis (supposedly) housing Alexander's sarcophagus at its heart. It was a port with two magnificent harbours and handled trade from the Red Sea as well as the Mediterranean. Its vast population, which in reaching an excess of 100,000 was the largest ever seen in a city to date, was highly cosmopolitan. With elite Macedonian Greeks, native Egyptians and Jews living in their own distinct quarters, the citizens were, for the most part, at least free to practise their beliefs and religious traditions within this open-minded metropolis.

Alexandria's celebrated lighthouse on the offshore island of Pharos, is thought to be the first purpose-built structure of its kind. Completed in the early third century BC at the behest of Ptolemy I, it stood marking the entrance of the harbour for over six hundred years. Its image was so synonymous with the city that it appeared on coins and

ABOVE: The now-lost lighthouse guided ships into the port of Alexandria. It was classed as one of the Wonders of the Ancient World.

in mosaics throughout that time. Then, in late antiquity, all references to this astonishing landmark ceased, and its demise, presumably due to some terrible natural disaster, continues to remain opaque and any remnants of it so far elusive.

The fate of another of Ptolemy's innovations at Alexandria, his Library, is no less murky. The Macedonian pharaoh was keen to make his capital into a beacon of intellectual life across the Mediterranean and invited the Athenian Demetrius of Phalerum to help him found a royal library and academy. Among those drawn to it was Euclid, 'the founder of geometry', while its head librarian, for a time, was Eratosthenes; a poet, critic and cartographer, who was among the first people to attempt to calculate the dimensions of the earth. Based in Syracuse, Archimedes was another thinker who drew succour and support from the Library for his innovative screw-shaped water pump among much else, and dedicated several of his published works to its librarians.

Though long rumoured to have been torched by Julius Caesar during his assault on the city in 47 BC, this now appears doubtful.

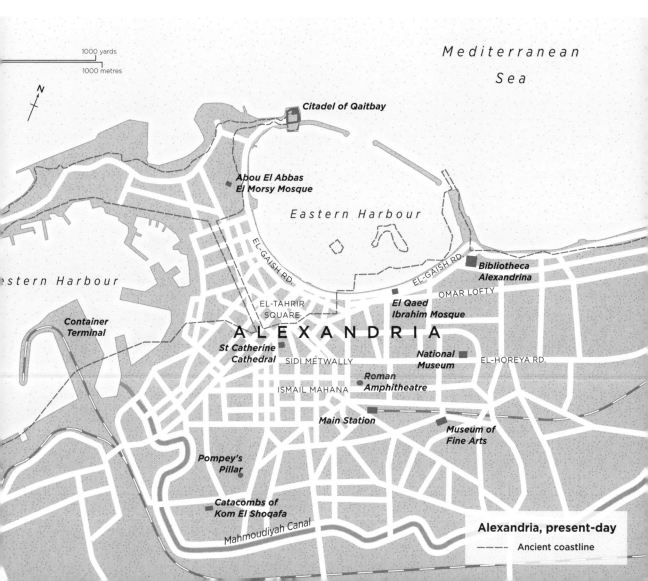

Alexandria, present-day
——— Ancient coastline

LEFT: Two statues recovered from the bottom of Alexandria's Eastern Harbour.

BELOW: Today the Citadel of Qaitbay sits on the original site of the lighthouse, on the Eastern Harbour.

Claudius Ptolemy, writing in Alexandria during the later reign of the Emperor Hadrian, appears to have been able to draw on a plethora of earlier books from the Library for his own studies of geometry and the Almagest. That there is no record of what finally became of it and its holdings, which almost definitely contained works by Aristotle lost forever, is an irony too bitter to contemplate. In 2004, however, archaeologists excavating in the Bruchion, or old Royal Greek area of the city, did uncover what looked like a complex of lecture halls dating from some 2,000 years ago that may possibly have formed part of the Library.

Whatever became of the Library (and the lighthouse for that matter), Alexandria was to continue as a place of importance during the centuries Egypt spent as a Roman province, even weathering, despite the destruction of temples dedicated to Serapis, the city's founding deity, the arrival of Christianity. It was, however, less able to cope with an earthquake in AD 365 that saw the ground sink beneath its grandest palatial districts, submerging a major part of ancient Alexandria permanently beneath the sea.

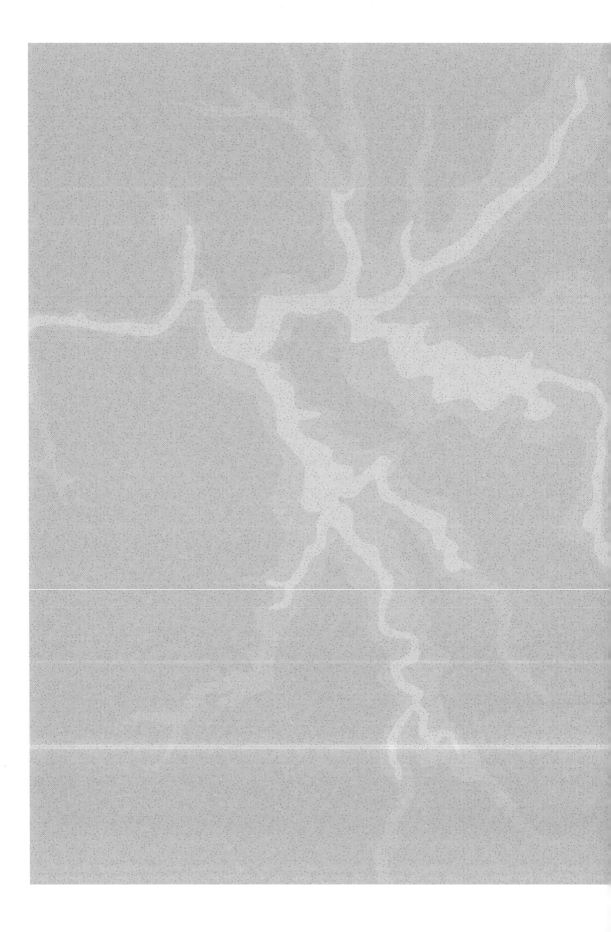

FORGOTTEN LANDS

CHAN CHAN

PERU

8° 06' 20.1" S / 79° 04' 28.7" W

By tradition Chan Chan's origins are traced back to a moment when a charismatic stranger, sailing from god knows where (but quite possibly a god himself), landed in a boat fashioned from reeds, the likes of which no one had seen before, on the shores of Trujillo in north-eastern Peru. Seemingly possessing a superior intelligence, this man 'from the other side of the sea', whose name was Tacaynamo, offered to educate the awestruck people on this corner of the Pacific coast in the ways of art, agriculture, irrigation, architecture, law and order and town planning. It was an offer that they deemed too good to refuse.

In all of these areas Tacaynamo emerged as more than an expert. And far from stinting in sharing his vast knowledge with others, the price demanded for receiving his pearls of wisdom was devoted worship, an utter fealty to his iron and infallible rule and the acceptance of an unyielding stratified society, with himself, naturally, right at the top.

This rigid order would come to be the defining feature of the Chimú civilization that was now to arise in this part of the Moche Valley and soon extended for over 600 miles (965km) from the south of Ecuador into central Peru. Hierarchical class distinctions were even baked into Chimú creation myths, with a metallurgically-minded sun god, having birthed the earth, creating its population from three eggs: one gold, one silver and one copper, and graded in the same manner as sporting prizes. It was also expressed most vividly and in physical form with the layout of Chan Chan, the great capital Tacaynamo is said to have willed into being.

With or without Tacaynamo, who in some versions of this rather convoluted foundation story is a monarch fleeing a bested earlier kingdom and who arrived with an entourage of loyal supporters all

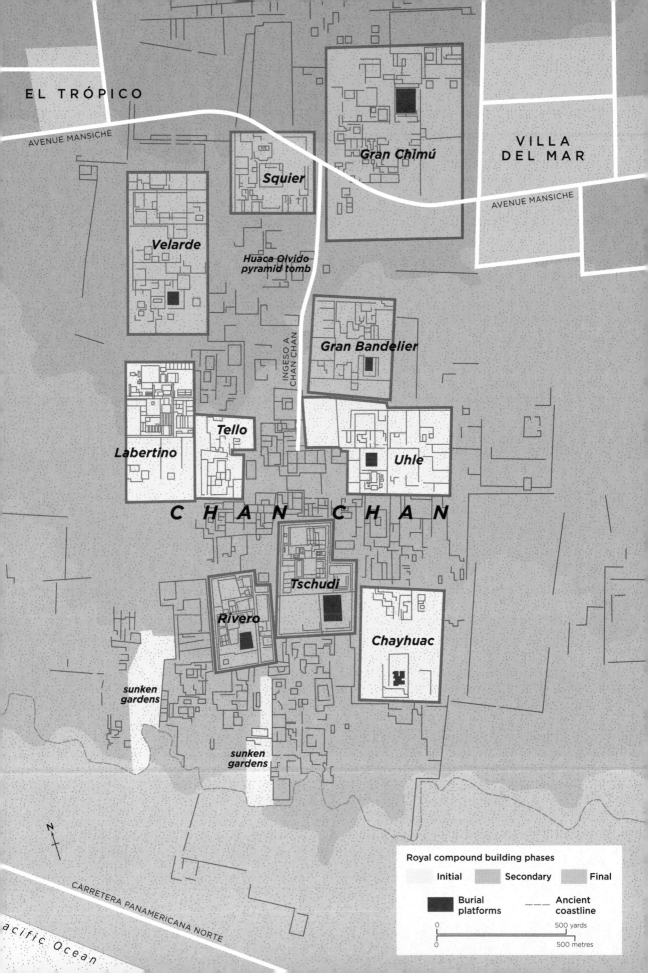

EL TRÓPICO

AVENUE MANSICHE

VILLA
DEL MAR

AVENUE MANSICHE

Gran Chimú

Squier

Velarde

*Huaca Olvido
pyramid tomb*

INGESO A CHAN CHAN

Gran Bandelier

Tello

Uhle

Labertino

C H A N   C H A N

Tschudi

Rivero

Chayhuac

*sunken
gardens*

*sunken
gardens*

N

CARRETERA PANAMERICANA NORTE

Pacific Ocean

Royal compound building phases

Initial   Secondary   Final

Burial
platforms

Ancient
coastline

0   500 yards

0   500 metres

intent on starting over again, Chan Chan would be the largest city in the Americas before the arrival of Europeans, and the greatest ever fashioned entirely in adobe. Commenced in about AD 850, Chan Chan was a monumental project in every sense – an earthen metropolis that finally occupied an area of nearly 8 square miles (20 square km) and was composed of nine (or ten in some accounts) autonomous citadel complexes. In each of these were royal palaces and temples with ornate friezes, and inner- and outer-walled courtyards, forums and rooms of state, with separate (and far from equal) quarters for priests, courtiers, servants and guards. Beyond, were heavily delineated service compounds and almost business-park-style manufacturing districts for workshops, gardens and farms. The whole thing operated not unlike a pre-Colombian American version of Downton Abbey, albeit on a vaster scale and with different dress codes. Chan Chan was home to at least 30,000 people – and that number, it has been suggested, perhaps nudged as high as 60,000 in its imperial pomp. The city was kept irrigated by a highly advanced system of channels, canals and wells – so highly advanced, in fact, that the Chimú have been hailed by UNESCO as 'the first true engineering society in the New World'.

Advanced engineering, however, proved no protection from the advance of the insurgent Incas who overran north Peru in around 1470. Chan Chan fell, was looted and partially destroyed, and time was called on the Chimú empire at a stroke. When the Spanish conquistador Francisco Pizarro arrived in 1532, the city was all but abandoned. Yet many of the buildings left standing retained ornate decorations exquisitely tooled in silver and gold. The conquistadores wasted no time in stripping Chan Chan of these accoutrements. And then, acting on the belief that Chimú nobles were often buried with their most prized possessions, began vandalizing whole sections of the city to obtain whatever precious metals might be hidden away in secret tombs, walls and passageways. Having extracted all they could find, the Spanish abandoned Chan Chan, leaving it to the mercy of the elements –the wind and the rain – whose relationship with mud-based buildings tends to the merciless.

Placed on UNESCO's list of World Heritage in Danger in 1986, and despite much valiant and ongoing conservation work to preserve the site since then, Chan Chan continues to deteriorate. The rate of decay has, depressingly, only worsened in recent years, with UNESCO judging in 2007 that the current levels of erosion are 'rapid and seemingly unstoppable'. Rising rainfall and the increasingly common El Niño storms – which only occurred every twenty to fifty years when Chan Chan was young but now rage across Peru with alarming frequency – are slowly but surely washing the city away.

RIGHT: Some of the statues on display at the Chan Chan Site Museum.

BELOW: The archaeological site of Chan Chan is made of earthen walled complexes.

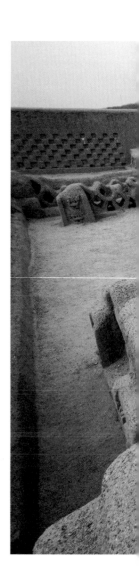

ROANOKE

NORTH CAROLINA, USA

35° 52' 53.3" N / 75° 39' 17.4" W

Since its founding governor John White was an artist and cartographer who left charts of the territory, delicately sketched in watercolour, you might think finding Roanoke would be easy. Yet the precise location of England's first serious stab at creating a colony in the New World of North America continues to be contested, and what befell its inhabitants after 1587 is an even greater mystery that after more than four centuries of speculation is no closer to being solved.

The story of Roanoke really begins back in 1577 when Sir Humphrey Gilbert, the parliamentarian, soldier, brutal colonizer of Ireland, seafaring adventurer and half-brother of Sir Walter Raleigh, submitted a proposal to Queen Elizabeth I entitled, 'How Her Majesty May Annoy the King of Spain'. In it, Gilbert argued that Protestant England needed to adopt a more belligerent stance against Catholic Spain. The Iberian nation had become a religious foe following the Pope's excommunication of Elizabeth in 1570 and was an increasingly troublesome commercial and maritime rival with substantial resources flowing in from its dominions in the Americas. Gilbert called for seizing the Spanish fishing fleet off Newfoundland near Canada, the occupation of Cuba and the interception of ships ferrying pilfered American treasures to Spain. Elizabeth dismissed almost all of Gilbert's suggestions but did grant him a charter to settle an English colony in the 'heathen lands not actually possessed of any Christian prince nor inhabited by Christian people' of North America. Gilbert would manage to annex the island of Newfoundland for Good Queen Bess – an act credited as the opening sally in the founding of the subsequent British Empire – but perished when his ship sank off the Azores in 1583 on the triumphant voyage home.

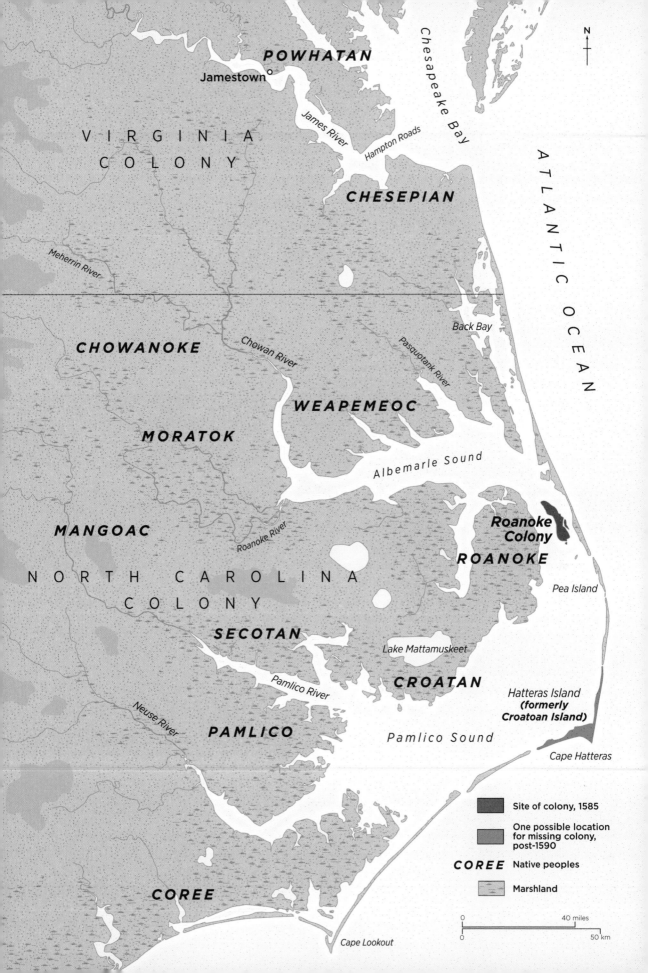

The baton of British colony-building then passed on to his kinsman, Sir Walter Raleigh, who dispatched two ships to explore the North Atlantic coast in April 1584. On 4 July, these vessels, captained by Philip Amadas and Arthur Barlowe and assisted by the experienced Portuguese-born pilot, Simon Fernandes, reached the shores of what is now North Carolina. After navigating their way through the treacherous inlets of the 'Outer Banks' they dropped anchor and went ashore to claim possession of these lands for England (and which were soon enough named Virginia, after the nation's Virgin Queen). After returning to England with two native Algonquian Americans they'd befriended called Manteo and Wanchese, and wildly enthusiastic reports about the region, in particular, an island called Roanoke, it was decided to send a fleet of seven ships back to Virginia and establish a permanent base there.

If initially successful in colonizing Roanoke, this second expedition was marred by difficulties and the colony proved short lived. There were intense personal disagreements between its leaders, Sir Richard Grenville and Sir Ralph Lane. The colonists were beset by a number of physical hardships with food becoming so scarce for one exploratory party that two mastiff dogs were killed and eaten and after which they were forced to subsist on 'a pottage of Sassafras leaves'. Perhaps worst of all there was an ominous and alarming deterioration in their relationships with the local American tribes. The latter situation was greatly exacerbated when the colonists torched a native village, most likely burning the last of that year's harvested corn in the process, in retaliation for the suspected theft of a silver cup. Leaving a standing force of fifteen men with two years' worth of supplies on Roanoke, the settlers finally cut their losses and headed back to England, where fresh schemes to secure the colony's future would be mulled over in the light of everything that had happened so far.

Armed, thanks to the second expedition's wider excursions in the surrounding territories, with a slightly better grasp of the local geography, questions began to be asked about whether Roanoke was really such an ideal place for a permanent colony after all. The inlets near the island were too narrow for larger ships to pass, making the establishment of a decent-sized harbour impossible. A location further north at Chesapeake Bay was suggested as a potentially more viable alternative. And it was to Chesapeake that the third expedition was supposed to be bound when it sailed from Plymouth in May 1587.

Unlike the previous all-male expeditions, the hundred-plus colonists on this voyage were comprised of both men and women, this mix of genders and ages a clear indication of the intention to sow more permanent seeds in America. Their new governor, John White, who despite being a veteran of the mostly disastrous second expedition, was enthusiastic enough about the colony's prospects that he persuaded his pregnant daughter, Eleanor, and son-in-law Ananias Dare to join the venture.

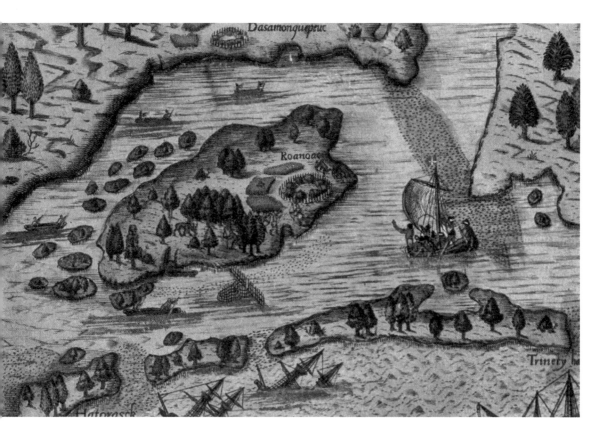

Dasamongueptuc

Roanoac

Trinety

Hatorask

ROANOKE

ABOVE: Illustration depicting the colony settling on Roanoke Island.

From here on in, certainties start to recede, with accounts left to us being slightly untrustworthily self-serving or downright contradictory. What we do know is that for reasons unknown, or motives corrupt and devious (and perhaps at the behest of Elizabethan spymasters), the pilot Simon Fernandes, who had assisted them on the 1584 expedition, refused to sail as far as Chesapeake and navigated to Roanoke, which they reached on 22 July 1587.

The colonists set about making the best of things, patching up what still stood of the original settlement and erecting new stockades, but did not clap eyes on any of the fifteen men left behind, and found just a few, possibly human bones scattered around. On 18 August 1587, there was much rejoicing when Eleanor Dare gave birth to a daughter, the first English child to be born in America and christened Virginia the following Sunday. But if this happy event did much to restore the spirits of the settlers, the arrival of a child (soon followed by another birth a few days later) only heightened an awareness of the vulnerability of their position. Here were two new mouths to be fed, and the colony's supplies were already looking limited in the face of the potentially bitter months of autumn and winter approaching. Largely against his will, White agreed to head back to England and return the following spring with more provisions and fresh recruits for the colony.

Sailing on 27 August 1587, he bid adieu to 119 men, women and children, among them his own daughter and nine-day old granddaughter, fully expecting to be back within a few months. But the war with Spain and other misfortunes prevented White from reaching America again for nearly three full years – and nothing further was heard about the colony in all that time.

Finally arriving within its vicinity, White was buoyed by the distant sight of smoke rising from the Island. But reaching the settlement on 18 August 1590, he discovered it completely deserted. (The smoke, it later emerged hailed from neighbouring natural bushfires.) Searching in vain for a hint of life or any clue as to what might have happened to the colonists, they found just the letters 'CRO' carved into the bark of a tree in 'faire Romane letters' and nearby a post inscribed with the word 'CROATOAN' in capitals. Since Croatoan was

an island some 50 miles (80km) south of Roanoke and peopled by a tribe of the same name, White concluded that the colonists must have headed there, after waiting month after desperate month for his failed return with the vital supplies. White could picture them sick and starving, scratching these letters into the wood in the hope he would eventually get the message and follow them there. But in this White would be thwarted too: stormy weather soon scuppered any further searches along the coast. The conditions grew so poor that the ship's captain insisted on charting a course back to the Caribbean, lest their vessel be sunk. In the event the crew hightailed it to England and White was never to see America again.

Nothing has ever been established about what truly became of the colonists of Roanoke; their more enduring British successors up the coast at Jamestown some twenty years later drew a blank, John Smith hearing only rumours from the natives about possible survivors allegedly living in places called Pakrakanick and Ocanahonan that continue to defy accurate location. (This is much like Roanoke itself, incidentally, since the erosion of the northern part of the island means that the ground where much of the original settlement most likely stood has succumbed to the tide of the rising sea.) In the centuries since, multiple theories, many of them lurid, have been posited about the settlers and these run the gamut from murder or abduction by native American tribes or slaughter at the hands of Spanish conquistadors, to the whole colony being wiped out by an epic tidal wave. Gentler accounts have them assimilating into Native American communities or merely drowning after embarking on a misguided attempt to reach England in the colony's remaining, and perhaps far from seaworthy, pinnace.

ABOVE: Recreation of the Croatoan tree carving at Fort Raleigh National Historic Site on Roanoke Island.

OPPOSITE: A replica 16th century sailing vessel at Roanoke Island Festival Park.

THE MOSQUE CITY
OF BAGERHAT

BANGLADESH

22° 40' 07.2" N / 89° 45' 19.0" E

It perhaps says as much about the legends surrounding Khan Jahan Ali – warrior, able and benevolent administrator, hydrologist, mosque builder and Sufi Muslim seer – that he is popularly held to have been conveyed to what is now Bagerhat on the backs of two crocodiles. Variously stated to be 'a Persian by birth', an Uzbek Turk, or of north Indian origin, Khan Jahan is thought to have been dispatched, with an army of followers (and with or without crocodiles), to what was then a remote and moribund corner of the continent's east coast in about 1398 by the Sultan of Delhi, Firuz Shah Tughlaq. His mission was to 'reclaim and cultivate the land' in this region, known as the Sundarbans and a delta dominated by mangrove swamps where the rivers Ganges and Brahmaputra converge and peter out into the sea of the Bay of Bengal. He was also charged with establishing an Islamic colony in this estuarial backwater.

Through personal charm, religious piety, superior organizational and leadership skills, and a practical knowledge of farming and engineering, he set about turning acres of tiger-infested jungle into rice fields. He laid down bridges and roads and embanked and diverted rivers to supply fresh water for irrigation and civic consumption to a new city called Khalifatabad, that he was building beside the Bhairab river. In keeping with the Sultan's second edict and Khan Jahan's own fervent faith, this elegant fortified metropolis was, by tradition at least, eventually supposed to have possessed some 360 mosques (fifty is believed to be nearer the mark).

After living as 'a great zamindar' (landowner), albeit one of extreme modesty who eschewed a royal title, Khan Jahan finally withdrew from 'worldly affairs' and spent his last years dwelling as a faqir. He died on

25 October 1459 and was buried in a single-domed mausoleum-cum-dargah (shrine) erected in the city at a site of his choosing, on the northern banks of a placid pond known as Thakur Dighi. (Until their own deaths in 2011 and 2014, two exceptionally elderly crocodiles, known, affectionately and respectively, as Dhalapahar and Kalapahar, and reputedly distant descendants of the reptiles that carried the great warrior saint here in the first place, kept vigil over these waters. Their place has since been taken by a fresh brood of crocodiles specially introduced for the purpose.)

Nevertheless, in the centuries after his death, Khalifatabad or Bagerhat as it would later come to be called, was abandoned and the jungle that Khan Jahan and his followers had so methodically tamed grew back, and more virulently than ever, with reeds, creepers and vines entwining themselves around the city's buildings and choking the life out of the place, as moss, algae and palm fronds invaded its lakes and ponds.

Surveyed in the 1890s, the dormant city would break out of this vegetative state in the opening years of the twentieth century, when the task of restoring some of its most significant buildings, among them some of the finest examples of early Islamic monuments and

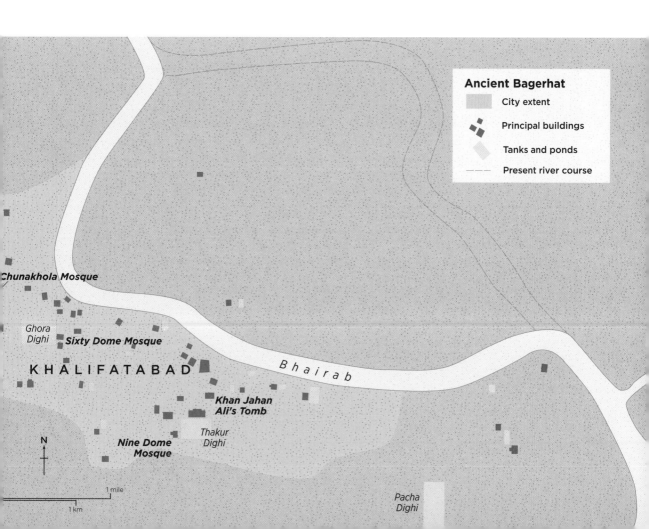

OPPOSITE TOP: The interior of the Sixty Dome Mosque shows the simplicity of the original design.

OPPOSITE BOTTOM: The exterior of the Sixty Dome Mosque with its bare brick facade.

brick-built mosques, was first begun. However, even today, many structures remain in advanced states of ruination, if perhaps given the surrounding landscape of jute fields and bamboo forests, rather romantically so. The Chunakhola Mosque, which in the words of one guidebook, 'has suffered heavily at the hands of the inclement weather of the area', remains decidedly picturesque to say the least. While the more extensively restored Nine Dome Mosque, and Shat Gombuj Masjid or Sixty Dome (or Column) Mosque, along with Khan Jahn's mausoleum, have a compellingly ascetic kind of grandeur, the simplicity of their original designs – with their bare brick facades and noble domes, only enhanced by the patina of age – and the decay, if fortunately arrested now, accrued through their years of neglect and isolation.

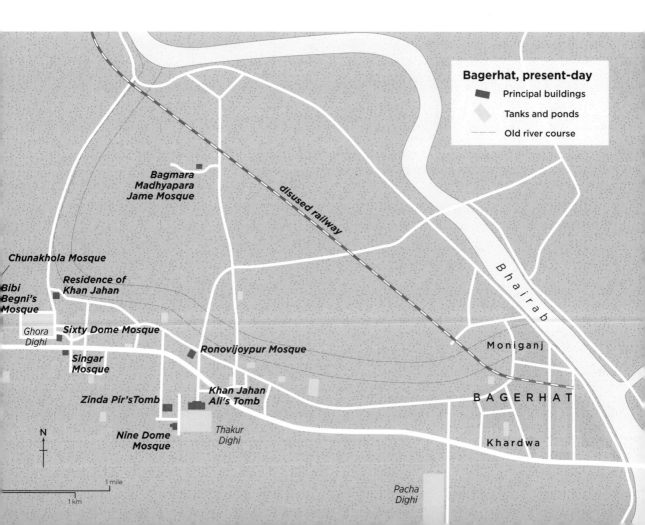

Bagerhat, present-day

Principal buildings

Tanks and ponds

Old river course

disused railway

Bhairab

Bagmara
Madhyapara
Jame Mosque

Chunakhola Mosque

Bibi Begni's Mosque

Residence of Khan Jahan

Ghora Dighi

Sixty Dome Mosque

Ronovijoypur Mosque

Moniganj

Singar Mosque

Zinda Pir'sTomb

Khan Jahan Ali's Tomb

BAGERHAT

Nine Dome Mosque

Thakur Dighi

Khardwa

N

1 mile

1 km

Pacha Dighi

RIVER FLEET

LONDON, UK

51° 30' 51.0" N / 0° 06' 17.7" W

If Angler's Lane, a little street that curves off the main thoroughfare of Kentish Town, has any real claim to fame it is that for over a hundred years it was home to the largest false-teeth factory in Europe. The red brick and terracotta building that formerly comprised the premises of Claudius Ash & Co. 'Manufacturers of False Teeth' from 1840 until 1965, still dominates the lane, though it has long since been converted into apartments. Ash was a silversmith who initially supplied the wealthy, if toothless, with dentures made from precious metals before pioneering 'mineral teeth'. This was an affordable alternative to the former and far more hygienic than other substitutes fashioned from wood or real human teeth extracted from both the living and the dead. But it was fishermen not false teeth that gave the lane its name. Before Victorian brickwork, paving and lead piping put paid to their sport, this quarter of north-west London was a haunt of anglers. Such rod wielders came to dip their lines and hooks in a freshwater fish-rich tributary of the River Fleet that flowed from its source in what was once the boggy, malarial marshlands of Hampstead down through what remained a largely pastoral Kentish Town and on into Camden Town and Kings Cross before passing by Clerkenwell to finally join the Thames at Blackfriars.

We still use the word 'fleet', which derives from the Old English *fēotan* meaning to 'float or swim' for a group of ships. But in Anglo-Saxon parlance it was also used quite specifically to refer to a tidal creek or inlet. For this reason, historically only the final part of the river was called the Fleet; its upper reaches were known as the Hole Bourne or Holborn (literally 'a stream in a hollow'), the River of Wells and the Turnmill Brook – the latter name a nod to the many watermills, at least four by the thirteenth century, that were erected

Highgate

Hampstead
Heath

Highgate
Cemetery

Highgate
Ponds

Hampstead
Ponds

Parliament
Hill

Holloway

mpstead

Kentish
Town

Belsize
Park

L   O   N   D   O   N

Primrose Hill

Camden
Town

Regent's Canal

Regent's
Park

King's Cross
Station

Islington

St Pancras
Station

Clerkenwell

Euston Station

Bloomsbury

Fitzrovia

Marylebone

Paddington
Station

Soho

Blackfriars Bridge

T h a m e s

N

Hyde
Park

Mayfair

Charing Cross
Station

on that section of the river. By then, however, the Fleet was evidently serving as something of an open sewer. The river was already so contaminated that in 1236 Henry II granted the citizens of London the right to divert waters from the Tyburn River in Westminster to the City through leaden pipes 'for the poore to drink'. In 1290 the White Friars, whose monastery lay to the west of the Fleet's Thameside mouth, filed a complaint about the appalling stench of the river. The smell was so bad, apparently, that even the monks' most pungent incense failed to mask it. The decision in 1343, to allow the butchers of Newgate Street to use one of the Fleet's waterside wharves to cleanse entrails can scarcely have improved things. Nor could the profusion of tanners who appear to have begun setting up shop beside the river around the same period and used its tide waters to treat their animal hides.

Whatever unsavoury items were floating about in the Fleet, its surface was often crowded with small boats ferrying goods and people upstream from the Thames. Thirteenth-century documents record

ABOVE: The River Fleet, which was once aboveground, flowing in front of Bridewell Palace.

masonry being shipped up shore on the river for the construction of the medieval St Paul's cathedral. Those seeking charity or treatment but too infirm or weak to walk were similarly conveyed to the doors of the Priory of St Bartholomew's Hospital, as were this medical establishment's supplies of corn and hay. While wine bound for the Fleet Prison, the grim debtors gaol destroyed in both the Peasants' Revolt of 1318 and the Gordon Riots of 1780, also travelled there by boat on its namesake. Among the other items conveyed in this manner include, in 1418, the stones for paving the streets of Holborn along with such victuals as oysters and herrings. Old Seacole Lane in modern Farringdon, meanwhile, memorializes the Fleet's role in the transport of sea-coal from Tyneside to London.

Still, as the population living outside the City walls grew, so too did the amount of rubbish and sewage dumped into the Fleet. Cleaned out once in 1502, and again in 1606, it was blocked up entirely once more by 1652, with one contemporary observer noting that it was 'impassable for boats, by reason of so many encroachments thereon made by the throwing of offal and other garbage by butchers, saucemen [a type of cook] and others by reason of the many houses of offices standing over upon it'. The lower part of the river was by this point also traversed by some five bridges, all of which, no doubt, offered further handily elevated vantage points from which to hurl stuff into the clogged water below.

However, during the blaze of the Great Fire of London in 1666, flames leaped from bank to bank incinerating wharves and houses on either side of the Fleet. In its wake, a new bridge was constructed over the river at Holborn to a design by Christopher Wren and in 1670 a scheme was undertaken (at some expense) to deepen and widen the river from this crossing to Blackfriars converting it into a new 15m (50ft) wide channel with capacious wharves. The 640 m (700yd) long Fleet Canal, as it was dubbed, proved financially unviable. What revenues the pitifully little traffic that brought it never offset its operating costs and it wasn't long before the canal became almost as rubbish-ridden as before. In 1733, the City authorities cut their losses and erected an arch over it. Six years later the old Stocks Market was removed to make way for the city's Mansion House building. A new market, the Fleet, was established on the archway where it remained until 1830 when this too was swept away by the laying for a new highway, Farringdon Road. Another victim of this highway would be the Fleet river itself, diverted underground into a pipe where it finally became a fully-fledged sewer, perhaps what it had been unofficially all along.

LION CITY

CHINA

29° 28' 57.6" N / 118° 45' 02.8" E

The lion is an ancient and universal symbol of bravery and strength. In China, reverence for these beasts is deep-seated; the lion is associated with regal power and is also believed to ward off evil spirits and herald good fortune. Highly stylized carved stone lions, known as 'fo dogs', are commonly found at the entrances to Chinese palaces and Buddhist temples and shrines, the lion having first been adopted as an early emblem of the faith in India. Usually these statues appear in pairs like guardsmen, with one lion depicted with a wide-open mouth and waggling tongue, and the other with its jaws closed and wearing an expression somewhere between pensive and menacing. Each symbolizes, respectively, the ancient Chinese concepts of yang and yin, the seemingly opposite but interdependent forces of life. And contrary as it might sound, there is a sense that Shi Cheng, or Lion City, lives on today largely because it died in 1959.

Lying some 248 miles (400km) to the south of Shanghai in Chun'an County in Zhejiang province and at the foot of the Five Lion Mountain, Shi Cheng was founded in the Tang dynasty around 1,300 years ago. Some of its most historic buildings date back to the second century AD. Growing to about half a square kilometre (124 acres) at its imperial peak, among its more striking architectural elements are the outer walls erected in the Ming period around the sixteenth century, its majestic five gateways and a further 265 archways, all heavily embellished with carvings and salutary of guardian lions, dragons and phoenixes.

Shi Cheng had age, beauty and inhabitants who could trace residency back generation after generation, but that cut no ice when it was decided to sacrifice the city along with at least six other towns

– over 1,000 villages and tens of thousands of acres of farmland – for the greater good of meeting the increasing demand for electricity in the larger urban centres of Shanghai and Hangzhou. In May 1954, Tan Zhenlin, the third secretary of the East China Bureau of the Communist Party of China Central Committee, announced the plan for a new hydropower development in Chun'an County that was to result in the creation of the Xin'anjiang Reservoir and Xin'an river hydroelectric station. It would also bring about the forced displacement of over 290,000 people.

The project was completed in 1959, and Shi Cheng disappeared beneath the newly manmade Qiandao Lake whose waters were to rise over 30m (100ft) high and inundate all that lay in the valley. For nearly fifty years Shi Cheng was almost entirely forgotten. It was not until 2001, and at the point when Communist China was joining the World Trade Organization, that divers exploring the lake were astonished to find an almost perfectly preserved city of wide-paved streets, temples and imposing walls. Its state of preservation was, in fact, almost eerie. With even wooden beams and stairs holding up, and the fresh water saving intricately decorated stonework that might easily have been despoiled by prolonged exposure to sand, sun and smoggy air, and much else above ground in the turbulent decades since the 1950s.

This 'Atlantis of the East', as it has been christened, has since become something of an aquatic tourist attraction, with underwater tours, limited to experienced divers, available during the summer months. Conscious of the potential risk posed to the city from visitors, the Chinese authorities have officially classified Shi Cheng as an historical relic. We can only pray that they succeed in finding a suitably yin-and-yang-like balance between satisfying the intense public interest in the site and preserving it.

BELOW: Qiandao Lake, the manmade, freshwater lake that flooded Shi Cheng.

LION CITY

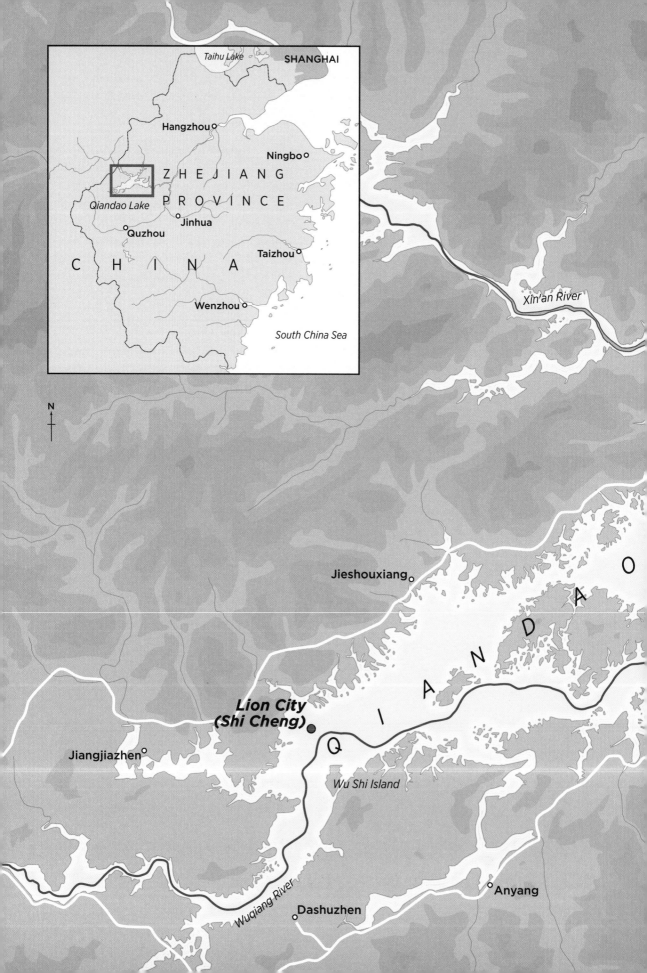

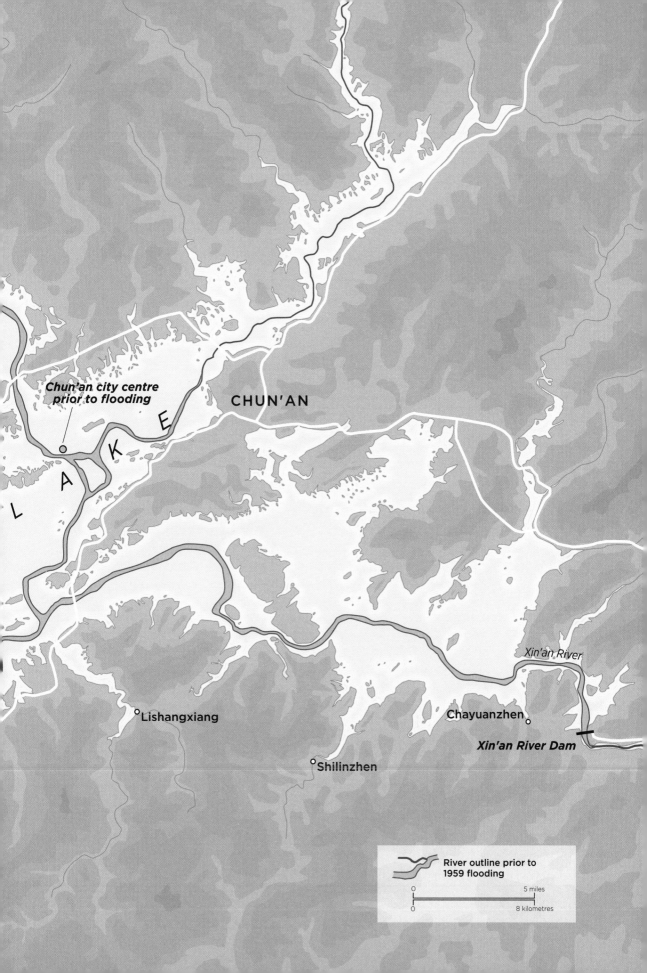

Chun'an city centre
prior to flooding

CHUN'AN

L A K E

Xin'an River

Lishangxiang

Chayuanzhen

Xin'an River Dam

Shilinzhen

River outline prior to
1959 flooding

0   5 miles

0   8 kilometres

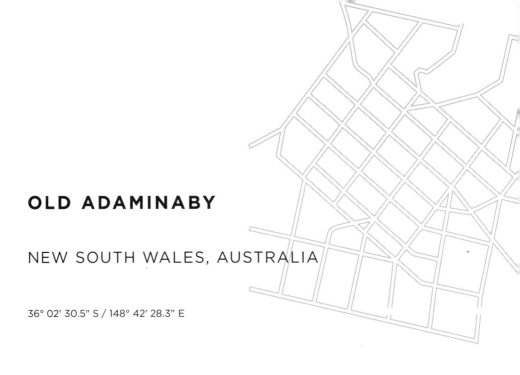

OLD ADAMINABY

NEW SOUTH WALES, AUSTRALIA

36° 02′ 30.5″ S / 148° 42′ 28.3″ E

Old Adaminaby was young once. There was a time before that, of course, when there was no town at all and the grassy plains of Monaro in the Eucumbene valley some 93 miles (150km) south of the modern Australian capital Canberra, were the preserve of the Ngarigo and Bemerangal peoples. The first European settlers did not arrive in this part of New South Wales until the 1820s, making Old Adaminaby, though scarcely born at this point, always an upstart in the grander scheme of things. Still, attracted by the possibility of rearing cattle on the vast tree-less tracts of open countryside nourished by the waters of Lake Eucumbene, a few pastoralists, cattlemen and horse breeders put down roots and odd travellers and prospectors looked in from time to time. The settlement was to receive a significant boost when in 1859 gold was discovered at Kiandra up in the Snowy Mountains 25 miles (40km) to its north east. With people flocking to Kiandra in their thousands, this near neighbour became a staging post and an enterprising stockman called Joseph Chalker opened a hotel in the hamlet to cater for those fortune seekers passing through. Two stores and a post office would soon follow, but so associated had the place now become with Joe's establishment that the town was known simply as 'Chalker's'. Such an arrangement, however, did not meet the approval of the surveyor for the Government Gazette who, after charting the region in 1861, took it upon himself to officially rename the town. He chose to call it Seymour, said to be his wife's maiden name. In any event, it was altered again in 1886 to Adaminaby to avoid confusion with another town of the same name in Victoria (though not, as far as can be ascertained, christened by the same surveyor).

If Kiandra's boom was brief, with the last mine closing in 1905, Adaminaby grew into a solid little town, its economy buoyed by the

Streets of the former
site of Adaminaby, *c.* 1940s

Present-day streets

1980 shoreline

Present-day shoreline

ANGLERS REACH ROAD

OLD ADAMINABY ROAD

STREET

CLANCY ST.

HILL ST.

BANJO ST.

LUCAS

Old Adaminaby

RAINBOW ST.

KIANDRA

COSGROVE

STREET

STREET

DENISON

caravan park

CHALKER

STREET

Township
Point

CAMP

STREET

STREET

BELL

GRAVE ST.

CROSS ST.

YORK

STREET

STREET

ALEXANDRA ST.

STREET

COOMA STREET

STREET

GORDON

HARNETT

STREET

LETT ST.

CATHCART

STREET

STREET

EDWARD STREET

SPRING STREET

FLAT STREET

EDEN STREET

BOLAIRA

STREET

SOUTH

L a k e   E u c u m b e n e

STREET

250 yards

250 metres

N

establishment of a butter factory and the opening of the nearby Kyloe Copper Mine. By the first decades of the twentieth century, there were five general stores, a court house, a couple of hotels, two schools, banks, churches, a hospital and doctor, along with a watchmaker, cafés, tearooms and a movie theatre, a showground and a race track. Its social and political life was diligently chronicled by a local newspaper and the town's weeks were punctuated by the balls and dances held without fail, and eagerly anticipated by young and old alike, every Friday and Saturday night. Winters might be 'harsh, cold wet and windy', as some later recalled, and heavy snowfall common enough, but such conditions only brought this close-knit community closer together. If its population remained relatively modest, reaching just 750 by the 1940s, and some of its facilities rather lagged behind larger urban towns as it stayed off the main gas, electricity, water and sanitation grids, it continued to be a beacon to the outlying rural districts. This in turn only added to Adaminaby's sense of itself as a place of importance locally. But almost a century to the day that Chalker's hotel opened shop, it was gone.

A scheme, long mooted in New South Wales, to divert and dam the Eucumbene river to help generate hydroelectric power, if largely leaving Adaminaby intact, was agreed in 1949 as part of Australia's bold post-war modernizing plans. That autumn the townsfolk even attended en masse a ceremony in a gorge on the river to celebrate its

BELOW: In 2007, the steps of St Mary's church were revealed by the receding water level of the Adaminaby dam.

commencement, where a charge was detonated and a plaque unveiled. That plaque, like the rest of Adaminaby, would wind up several feet below water when, after further research, a new dam design that extracted greater power, if unfortunately flooding more of the Eucumbene valley, was adopted instead.

The government, sensitive at least to the issue of uprooting a community, members of which had farmed the land and raised cattle here for four generations, offered a resettlement plan. Not only would another Adaminaby, and one rigged up with all the benefits of modern plumbing and electric power, arise at a safe distance from the dam water; they would move, brick by brick, clapboard by clapboard, about a hundred of the old town's buildings, among them two churches, to this new location. This work would begin in 1956, though the re-directed lake would not reach its full capacity until 1973 with many old town residents bitterly opposing their enforced displacement until the bitter end well before then. Over half those who did move to new Adaminaby, left almost immediately, complaining of the unexpected added expense of on-tap amenities, the lack of outside space to keep their customary horses and cows, and poor job prospects.

In time, water sports on the enlarged lake and skiing on the snowy peaks would bring tourists to the region, compensating, financially if nothing else, for the loss of fine pastures and cattle-rearing grounds hereabout. But as long ago as the 1980s, old Adaminaby began rearing its forlorn head, as the lake's water level started to deplete due to environmental changes. The ghost of this condemned town finally manifested itself with a vengeance in 2007 with the arrival of the worst drought on record for a hundred years. With the lake down to 10 per cent of its normal coverage the remnants of the town were fully revealed for the first time in nearly half a century. But as if to add further indignity to its initial disappearance, looters made off with newly exposed historic farm equipment and even parts of entire buildings. Thanks to the agitation of local community groups, in 2008 a heritage preservation order was passed, imposing hefty fines on anyone who sought to remove anything from old Adaminaby. In the meantime, the lake has since stabilized to around 20 per cent of its earlier height. For the moment, the old town sits in a curious limbo, lost and found, dead yet alive, a rebuke from the past about heavy-handed planning of yesteryear that also pleads for more to be done in the years to come.

PORT ROYAL

JAMAICA

17° 56' 12.4" N / 76° 50' 29.3" W

As one history of the place puts it, 'Port Royal is today a singularly unspectacular little town.' Its unspectacular-ness is all the more extraordinary given just how spectacular it once was. Though spectacular doesn't quite convey what exactly this sleepy fishing village of 1,600 residents perched on a sand spur in the mouth of Kingston Bay was once so famous, or, perhaps more accurately, notorious for.

A small clue is provided in the name of the local hotel, Morgan's Harbour. This genteel enough establishment caters to those few tourists who venture here either to take advantage of the excellent marlin fishing or to seek out what little remains of Port Royal from the era when Captain Henry Morgan called it home. Morgan was a Welsh farmer turned ruthless Caribbean privateer who raided Spain's American colonies and sacked Panama before being knighted and made Lieutenant Governor of Jamaica.

At that time, in the late seventeenth century, plenty of other people had other names for Port Royal; most were far from homely. Ranging from 'The Dunghill of the Universe' to 'The Wickedest City on Earth', none of them conveyed the idea of cosiness or somewhere to lay one's hat after an honest day's toil; quite the opposite in fact. This was hardly surprising since the town was a freebooter's paradise, a British-run Caribbean hot spot where pox-ridden and sunstroke-touched buccaneers could legally offload the loot plundered from Spanish galleons, and then avail themselves of the taverns and brothels that reputedly made up a quarter of all the premises.

But this 'Godless' Sodom and Gomorrah of maritime excess was the direct, if unintended, consequence of Oliver Cromwell's 'Western Design' campaign. This was an audacious scheme dreamt up by the Lord Protector in the wake of his conquest of Catholic Ireland to plant

English Parliamentarian protestantism in the Americas by seizing territories in the West Indies held by popish Spain. In 1654, Cromwell dispatched a massive armada helmed by Admiral William Penn and General Robert Venables, commanders-in-chief, respectively, of the navy and army, to claim Hispaniola for Britain. Ignominiously repulsed by superior Spanish forces at Santo Domingo, the English retreated into Kingston Bay on 10 May 1655, where, with Penn and Venables fearing the consequences of returning to the Protector empty handed, they fell upon on the more scantily occupied and far less well defended Jamaica with a vengeance. Carrying it off initially as a kind of consolation prize, having managed to overcome the Spanish militia, the English, battle weary and plagued with dysentery, began consolidating their position on the island. Alongside buildings, they erected a defensive stone fort named after Cromwell on the westernmost point of a spur that formed a natural harbour.

Known to the English as Point Cagway, and reserved by the Spanish as an area for careening ships, it had previously served for centuries as

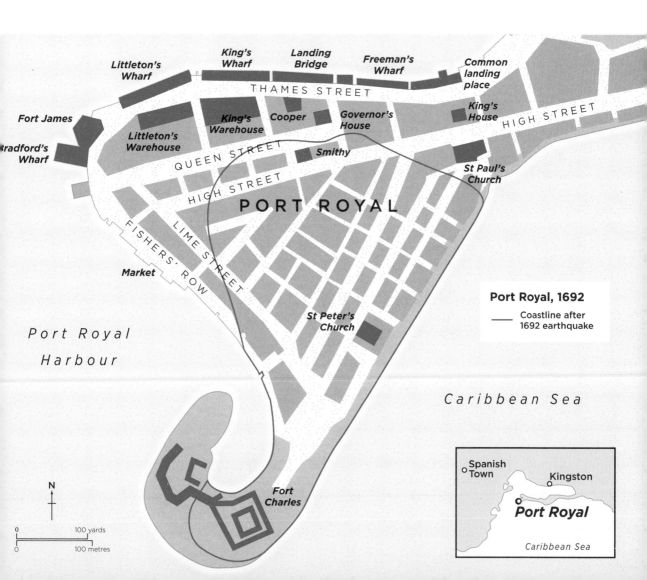

a fishing port for the Taínos people. Jamaica's earliest inhabitants, the Taínos were to suffer doubly from their encounters with the Spaniards who first arrived with Christopher Columbus in 1494. Slaughtered in their hundreds by sword- and musket-happy conquistadors, and then forced into slave labour, the numbers of Taínos were even more severely depleted by exposure to common European diseases to which they had no immunity. Indeed, the subsequent absence of much of an indigenous population to exploit would duly result in the wholesale importation of enslaved Africans to Jamaica, first by the Spanish and then the British.

In the earliest years of the English colony, simply retaining control of the island was the most pressing concern. In 1657, with the bulk of the original invasion fleet returned to Britain and many of the remaining vessels far from battle worthy, the Governor Edward D'Oyley chose to turn to perhaps a rather unusual quarter for help in preventing the Spanish from regaining possession. Aware that gangs of English and French pirates, holed up in the wild lands of the northern shores of Hispaniola and on the island of Tortuga, were carrying out sorties against Spanish ships travelling on the Windward Passage between Cuba and what is modern-day Haiti, he invited them to come to Jamaica and put up at the Point.

Lying at the heart of the Caribbean Sea, the island had distinct locational advantages for those wishing to pick off ships laden with treasure (gold, spices, tobacco and timber) travelling from the Spanish Main back to Cadiz. But here, too, and on the tacit understanding that they might offer some naval muscle down the line, the pirates were given the opportunity to legitimately dispose of booty obtained from enemy (Spanish) ships and territories under a dubious prize court system that also usefully boosted the colony's coffers. In addition, they might even be given commissions or letters of marque by D'Oyley as 'privateers' to conduct specific raids on certain alien vessels or terrains. Alongside this, a fine harbour was at their disposal, one where ships could be patched up, skull-and-crossbones flags darned and fresh provisions taken on board as future voyages were plotted. Around the town itself, there was to be an increasing range of divertingly pleasant, if largely intoxicating and/or potentially infectious, things they could spend their ill-earned money on.

Of course, there were moments when, as one chronicler put it, the pirates 'were ... disinclined to distinguish between an enemy vessel and an English one, when the chance of a prize offered itself'. D'Oyley had little by way of guarantee that if push came to shove and the Spanish mounted a full-scale assault, such marauders wouldn't just splice their mainbraces and sail off into the sunset, with a yo-ho-ho and a bottle of rum, at the first opportunity. Yet it seems clear that their presence did quell guerrilla action from the few Spaniards and their sympathizers left on the island. More importantly, it deterred an all-out invasion and, for good or ill, was to ensure the long-term future of the colony.

It did, however, mean that trade in this formative period consisted 'principally in plate, money, jewels and other things brought in by privateers', as one landowner grouched in 1669. Such men of property were looking for a more sustainable future for Jamaica based around agriculture. This planting interest would grow in power and wealth as the steady profits from sugar cane farmed with slave labour rapidly started to exceed the easy, if uneven, spoils obtainable from petty nautical larceny. The restoration of the English monarchy and the crowning of Charles II, which was to see Fort Cromwell hastily renamed Fort Charles and the Point become Port Royal, was also to cause a shift in geo-political loyalties. A brief accord with Spain technically rendered its boats out of bounds to British privateers, but even while this fragile and short-lived peace lasted, the local privateers appear to have paid little heed to such diplomatic niceties.

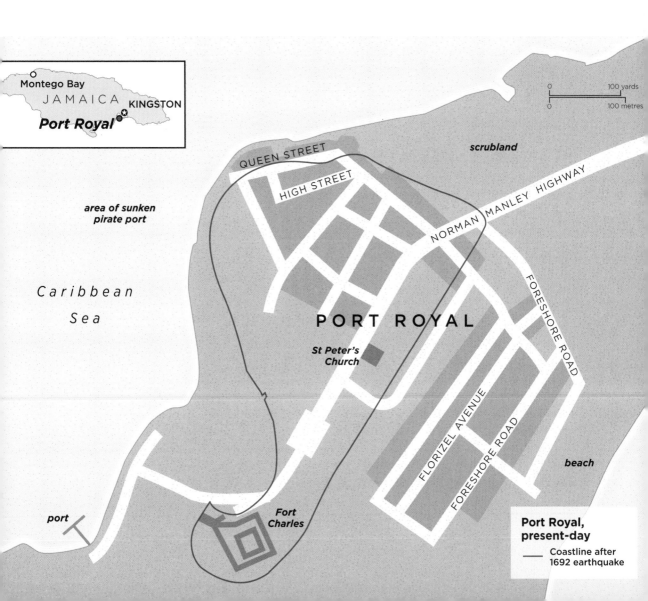

Montego Bay
JAMAICA KINGSTON
Port Royal

scrubland

QUEEN STREET

HIGH STREET

NORMAN MANLEY HIGHWAY

area of sunken
pirate port

Caribbean
Sea

PORT ROYAL

FORESHORE ROAD

St Peter's
Church

FLORIZEL AVENUE

FORESHORE ROAD

beach

port

Fort
Charles

**Port Royal,
present-day**

—— Coastline after
1692 earthquake

In the end, however, what terminated Port Royal's glorious reign as the roistering capital of the Caribbean was an earthquake that the religiously minded took as a sign from God.

On Wednesday, 7 June 1692, the whole of Jamaica was rocked by violent tremors but Port Royal was hit far worse, with the ground cracking open all over the place and a tidal wave then rushing through the town as whole streets of buildings collapsed. A church to the east crumbled and promptly slipped into the ocean with the ease of a sachet of sugar being tipped into a cup of coffee.

A witness left this account of the devastation: 'The sand in the street rose like waves of the sea, lifting up all persons that stood upon it, and immediately dropping down into pits; and at the same instant a flood of water rushed in, throwing down all who were in its way; some were seen catching hold of beams and rafters of houses, others are found in the sand that appeared when the water drained away with their legs and arms out.'

Whereas the earthquake claimed the lives of just fifty people across the rest of the island, some 2,000 of Port Royal's 6,000-odd population perished during the earthquake itself. But as many of the survivors were left damp and without shelter or fresh water, a further 2,000 would die in the aftermath from malignant fevers and other maladies. Since the quake cracked open the town's graveyard, bringing the bodies to the surface, the flood waters bobbed with corpses both fresh and long-festering, something that only added to the insanitary conditions for those left alive.

Now reduced to a rump of a mere 100 square metres (25 acres), Port Royal was rebuilt but it was to lose ground as the main seat of trade and politicking to the emerging town of Kingston. Disaster struck again in January 1703 when a fire swept through Port Royal destroying virtually everything but the castle. Visited by a hurricane that did for most of the ships in the harbour on 28 August 1712, it was dealt a fatal blow exactly a decade later when 'a dreadful storm' arrived on 28 August 1722 and proceeded to 'split the castle' and 'lay the church and two-thirds of town flat', killing 400 people.

After this Port Royal would be repurposed as a British naval station, one manned for a time by a young Horatio Nelson, that endured into the twentieth century. But out beyond the bay and not far below the surface of the sea lie the streets and buildings where pirates got blind drunk on pipes of wine, often spending as much as 3,000 pieces of eight in a night. Beyond that, too, in the murk and mud of the ocean bed, are estimated to be the largest single collection of wrecks in the world. Vessels, some sunk for refusing to give up their precious treasure three hundred years ago, are slowly being excavated. The wealth of artefacts unearthed in more recent years only confirm just how extraordinary a place Port Royal once was.

BELOW: Port Royal Street, Kingston after an earthquake in 1907, showing Jamaica is still prone to this natural disaster.

ESANBEHANAKITAKOJIMA

JAPAN

45° 19′ 53.8″ N / 142° 10′ 55.0″ E

In 2016 a British manufacturer of nametags conducted a survey of commonly lost items, as you probably would do if your business depended on peddling the kind of labels that aim to prevent clothing going astray in the scrum of school changing rooms, or luggage on fraught international flights. Topping its poll were keys, devices, in a sense, largely intended to help stop other stuff going awol by securing homes from burglars or vehicles from theft. Not far behind them, however, were mobile phones, lipsticks, pairs of glasses, remote controls and gloves, all of which enjoyed honourable placings in its '20 most lost' list. Of those people surveyed, around two thirds admitted they 'regularly' lost things and on average most people confessed to misplacing around four items a month. Of the larger items to go missing were cars. Though for the most part these seemingly only vanished 'temporarily' and largely through their owners either forgetting for a time exactly where they had parked them or simply, if briefly, being unable to recognize their own cars amid lots packed with many similar-looking vehicles. (Quite how drivers managed in the golden age of the one-colour, one-style, black Ford Model-T is a mystery of history, obviously.)

Another element that comes across from the survey is the degree to which many of its respondents had often remained cheerily oblivious to their loss until said absent items were required. The favourite scarf, for instance, assumed safely stashed in the wardrobe through the warm days of summer, and only sought out as the leaves redden and the days darken, is then mysteriously nowhere to be found, and so on. And something rather similar occurred in the case of the islet of Esanbehanakitakojima in Japan.

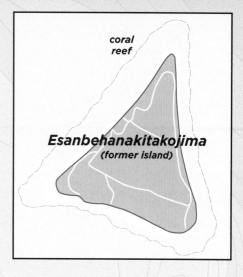

coral reef

Esanbehanakitakojima
(former island)

S e a   o f   O k h o t s k

Esanbehanakitakojima
(see above)

SARUFUTSU

fishing port

industrial units

CHINA

RUSSIA

Kuril Islands
(disputed)

Esanbehanakitakojima

Vladivostok

NORTH
KOREA

Sapporo *Hokkaido*

*Sea of
Japan*

SOUTH
KOREA

★ TOKYO

J A P A N

Pacific Ocean

N

N

0   500 yards
0   500 metres

For as long as anyone could remember, there'd been a small island lying roughly 500m (550yd) off the coast from Sarufutsu village on the northern tip of Hokkaido. It wasn't much to write home about, and was less uninhabited than almost entirely uninhabitable by humans; a truly unwelcoming, frigid, wind- and snow-lashed piece of rock. Yet it was considered important enough to be officially named in 2014 along with another 157 similar outlying islands that would consequently define Japan's territorial waters. This action was taken to clarify the extent of the nation's dominions against incursions in the Pacific from an expansionist China, and over long-standing disputes with its other major regional neighbour, Russia. Since the end of the Second World War when Soviet forces advanced to claim parts of Imperial Japan nearest its shores, the Russians have occupied the Kuril Islands. This archipelago sits not so far beyond Esanbehanakitakojima, and Japan still believes it is rightfully theirs.

Of Esanbehanakitakojima itself, Sarufutsu fisherfolk would recall giving the islet a wide berth. But their views on the island were only canvassed in the autumn of 2018 after it was found to have gone missing, having vanished completely unnoticed and with all the ease of a coin slipping down the back of a sofa. Its disappearance might have gone unnoticed for even longer (though the precise date of its loss remains hazy) had Hiroshi Shimizu not been looking for it. The journalist and author of an illustrated book on Japan's hidden islands, Shimizu was researching a second volume on the same theme and travelled to Sarufutsu in September 2018 to get acquainted with an islet lying offshore. Arriving in this most northerly corner of Japan, he headed for the shoreline armed with a map of where Esanbehanakitakojima was supposed to be. But no matter how long or hard he looked out at the chilly waters of the Sea of Okhotsk, there appeared to be no trace of the island. He sought the help of the local fishing fleet, but their excursions out into the ocean and consultations of well-worn local charts, only confirmed his fears; Esanbehanakitakojima had gone.

He contacted the Japanese Coast Guard who revealed that the last time Esanbehanakitakojima had been formally surveyed was in 1987. Back then the islet was recorded as jutting a mere 1.4m (4½ft) above normal sea level and in the following year a map based on this information was created by the Geospatial Information Authority of Japan.

In the intervening thirty years, the islet would have been exposed to all manner of natural forces that might have caused it to disappear. Buffeted by storm waves, strong winds and drifting ice, it's possible that Esanbehanakitakojima was eroded away over time or that its surface area has gradually sunk beneath rising sea levels.

ABOVE: Esanbehanakitakojima may have disappeared beneath the stormy waters of the Sea of Okhotsk.

For a land comprised of main four islands, Hokkaido, Honshu, Shikoku and Kyushu, and whose national identity and watery limits are bound up with islands, the loss of Esanbehanakitakojima, whatever its actual scale (and in comparison to its decidedly lengthy name), is no small thing. It also may spell the potential loss of some 500m (550yd) of Japanese territory and require the re-drawing of the odd map or two.

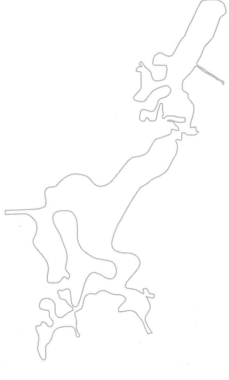

THE LOST SEA

CRAIGHEAD CAVERNS, TENNESSEE, USA

35° 32' 08.0" N / 84° 25' 51.9" W

Craighead Caverns have an impressively long history when it comes to being lost, and then to being found. The first known case of misplacement in these caves deep in the foothills of the Great Smoky Mountains on the Appalachian chain in East Tennessee can reasonably be traced back to at least 20,000 years ago. That was during the last Ice Age in the Pleistocene epoch; a period when Greenland, Canada and parts of North America were submerged beneath shifting glaciers. While dinosaurs were long gone, their extinction pegged to the end of the Cretaceous period some 66 million years ago, megafauna – huge mammals such as the woolly mammoth, the sabre-toothed cat, the Meglaoceros or giant deer, and the glyptodont, a car-sized armadillo – still roamed the earth. Though, increasingly, alas, on borrowed time.

Among the oversized species not to survive the passing of the Pleistocene was *Panthera onca augusta* or the giant jaguar, a larger forerunner of the modern jaguar that was endemic to North America and most definitely prowling around Tennessee. Around 10,000 years before their eventual extinction, one giant jaguar wandered into the Craighead Caverns. Perhaps to evade a predator or simply seeking shelter, it went deeper and deeper into the caves before seemingly losing its way and falling into a crevice. Paw marks left by this unfortunate creature and its near-complete skeleton were found in 1939. The specimen is on permanent display in the American Museum of Natural History in New York, while plaster casts of the paw marks can be viewed in Craighead Caverns' visitor centre.

By the time this big cat's remains were discovered, the caves had already acquired a certain notoriety. Located in the heart of Cherokee

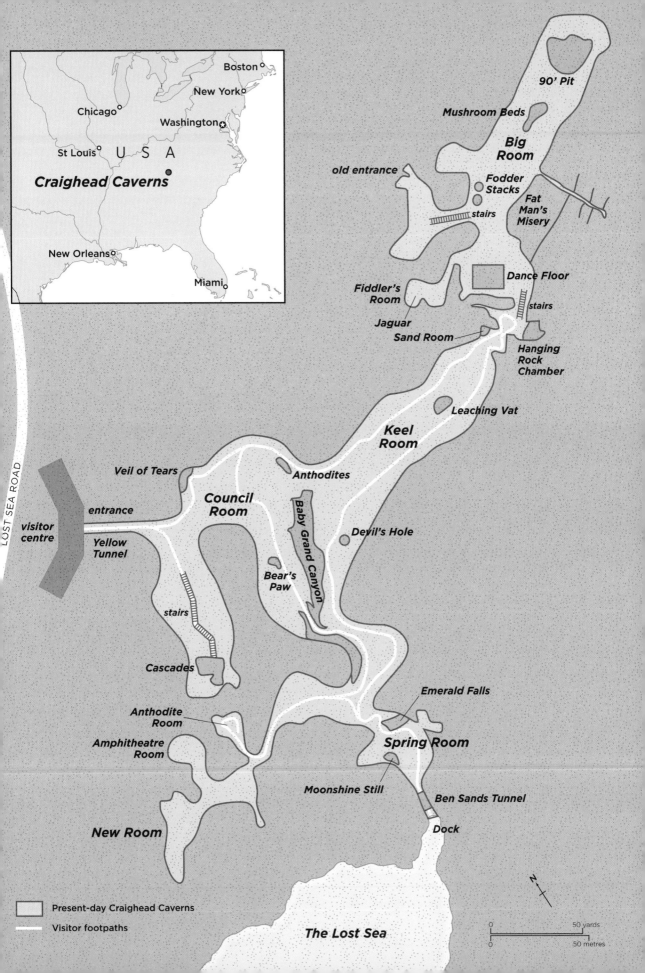

Indian country, they'd been utilized as a larder by the first white settlers to encroach on the territory in the 1820s and were mined by the Confederate Army for saltpetre, the main ingredient in gun powder, during the American Civil War. Their cool, out-of-sight interiors, meanwhile, also found favour with bootleggers who used the darker recesses to store their illegal stills of moonshine – the raw whiskey distilled from corn, barley and rye that is something of an Appalachian speciality. The earliest attempts to turn the caves into a place of resort included the installation of the dance floor and the staging of cock fights.

But the caves' greater fame was finally to rest on another piece of prehistory that had, in effect, gone missing for a while: a whole lost sea. Until around 65 million years ago all of what is now Tennessee had been under the ocean. But shifts in the Earth's tectonics caused the floor to rise, bringing the layers of limestone – the sedimentary rock composed of skeletal remains of marine organisms – to the surface. These caverns were the result of groundwater seeping down

through this soft rock over time, and at the lowest level, some 43m (140ft) underground, is a cave full of crystal-clear water that formed some 20,000 years ago. This lost sea, or lake, to be precise, would have to wait until 1905 before anyone found it. And that someone was a 13-year-old boy called Ben Sands, who had previously explored the caves with his father. On this particular day, he crawled alone through a 90m (300ft) long passage and reached a chamber that looked to contain a large pool of water. Throwing rocks and mud out into the far distance all that greeted him was the sound of splashes as they hit the water but not of reaching the bottom. What he had chanced upon was America's largest underground lake, the full extent of which has yet to be mapped and whose bottom still has not been reached by scuba divers. Currently some 53 square metres (13 acres) of the Lost Sea have been charted, how much more remains to be explored is a matter of speculation. But since 1965, when the caves were opened as a fully-fledged attraction with new entranceways and modern facilities and no shortage of signage, they've been pretty easy to find.

BELOW: The Lost Sea inside the Craighead Caverns.

BODIE

CALIFORNIA, USA

38° 12' 41.7" N / 119° 00' 45.3" W

Old wild western ghost towns don't come much ghostlier than Bodie. And in the days of the old west, few surpassed this mining town on the eastern foothills of the Sierra mountains for wildness either. Such a byword for lawlessness did it become that the phrase 'a Bad Man from Bodie' was used indiscriminately to describe almost any unidentified maleficent gunslinger or stagecoach robber in the west for a time.

The town had been named after one W.S. Bodey. Said to be either 'a Mohawk Dutchman' or 'a Scot', but by all accounts a compact fellow standing at around 1.7m (5ft 6in), Bodey was typical of the thousands of tin-pot prospectors who rushed to this part of California after hearing of the discovery of gold at Sutter's Mill near Coloma in 1848. Eleven years later and while panning for placer deposits at Taylor Gulch on the eastern side of the Sierra range, Bodey and his companions struck lucky. Unfortunately for Bodey, he was to perish in a blizzard in 1860 before getting to savour the spoils of this particular find. Out of reverence for their fallen, fellow prospector – a guy like themselves seeking to make an easy fortune the hard way – the mining camp became known as 'Bodey's Place', and the name stuck as it grew in size. The change in spelling is attributed to a slapdash sign-writer's error.

Nevertheless, with gold nuggets initially rather thin on the ground, Bodie stayed a modest encampment. By the mid-1860s there were still no more than fifty residents and its real estate consisted of just twenty wood and adobe shacks and a boarding house/saloon. All that was to change in 1875 when the mine at Bunker Hill collapsed exposing rich deposits of the ore. Overnight Bodie boomed, and with word soon reaching San Francisco, speculators from all over the west upped their picks and headed to the town, all intent on grabbing a piece of the

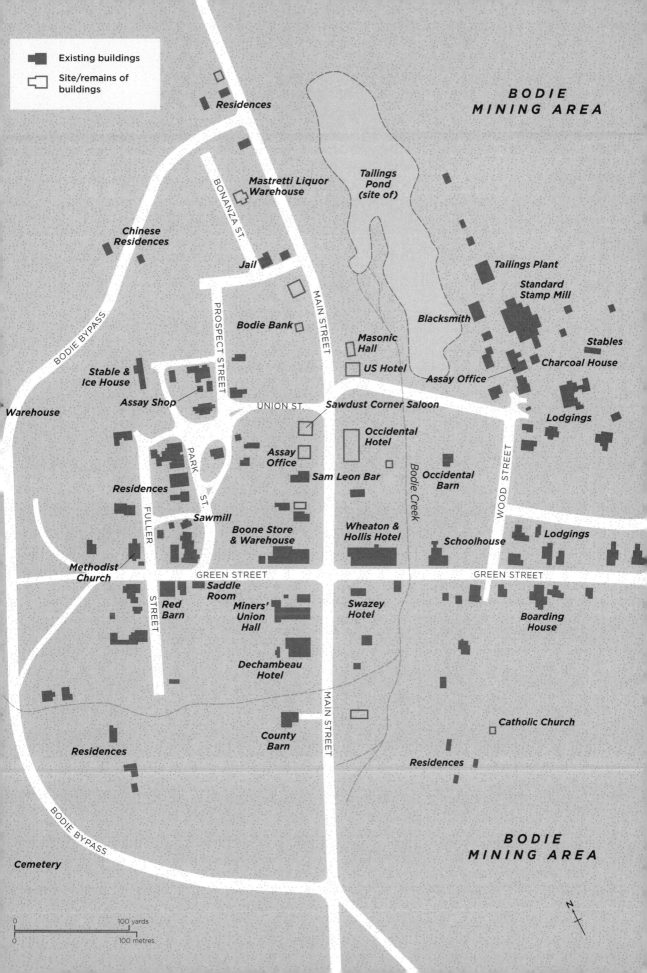

Existing buildings

Site/remains of buildings

Residences

BODIE
MINING AREA

*Mastretti Liquor
Warehouse*

*Tailings
Pond
(site of)*

BONANZA ST.

*Chinese
Residences*

Jail

Tailings Plant

*Standard
Stamp Mill*

Blacksmith

Stables

Bodie Bank

*Masonic
Hall*

US Hotel

Assay Office

Charcoal House

BODIE BYPASS

PROSPECT STREET

MAIN STREET

*Stable &
Ice House*

Assay Shop

UNION ST.

Sawdust Corner Saloon

Lodgings

Warehouse

*Assay
Office*

*Occidental
Hotel*

Sam Leon Bar

Bodie Creek

*Occidental
Barn*

WOOD STREET

PARK

Residences

ST.

Sawmill

*Boone Store
& Warehouse*

*Wheaton &
Hollis Hotel*

Schoolhouse

Lodgings

FULLER

*Methodist
Church*

GREEN STREET

GREEN STREET

*Boarding
House*

STREET

*Red
Barn*

*Saddle
Room*

*Miners'
Union
Hall*

*Swazey
Hotel*

*Dechambeau
Hotel*

MAIN STREET

Catholic Church

Residences

*County
Barn*

Residences

BODIE BYPASS

BODIE
MINING AREA

Cemetery

N

0   100 yards

0   100 metres

action or turning a buck on the side. For where gold diggers went there were plenty of others seeking to relieve them of their gains. It wasn't long before Bodie's Main Street was lined with stores, saloons and gambling dens. The town acquired Chinese opium dens and a red-light district admired for the superior quality of the girls – some of whom, such as the fabled Rosa May, a tart with a heart of a gold and a purse quite full of it too, passed into local legend. Tellingly perhaps, prostitution wasn't outlawed in California until 1910, while opium was outlawed far earlier, with punitive new laws passed against running, and even visiting, dens passed in 1881.

Gold mining is, in any case, gruelling, dreary and thirst-making work. Something like 90 per cent of gold rush prospectors are calculated to have been male. Who then can really blame them for wanting to kick back with a Scotch or a beer, play some cards, and seek the embrace of another, or the oblivion of the poppy pipe, after a day of breaking rocks. But almost inevitably in a town inhabited by armed, and not infrequently inebriated transients, some 'madder and badder' to tangle with than others, violent crime was a fact of life.

Writing in 1878, Joseph Wasson was to claim that 'as a general thing the town' was 'not an unruly one', though since a 'street duel' in the 'previous fall to last fall ... wherein two principals were shot to death', he did concede that 'sallies with sidearms ... with serious results' had been occurring rather more frequently.

Two years later Bodie was at its height with an estimated 8,000–10,000 inhabitants, the exact figure hard to calculate due to the ever-shifting make up of its population. It had also become notorious as a festering godless hell-hole of sin and corruption; a low town where no good man was to be found and no decent woman should venture unless she wished to be lured into vice. Or so certain newspapers happily maintained. And some folk in town didn't exactly mind its bad press, even seeing it as something of a badge of honour to survive in such a rough and tumble kind of place.

Towards the end of the 1880s, though, stocks of gold waned and with them went Bodie's roving bands of fortune seekers. By 1890, it was calmer and quieter; a community of a mere 682 souls, some of them families, able to take their pick of the two new churches that had recently been built. The mining of marginal ore and a cyanide plant provided gainful employment for the next forty years or so but, with their closure after the Second World War, Bodie was robbed of its purpose and most of its few remaining inhabitants.

Gradually it settled into becoming a kind of macabre spectre of its former self. Shacks crumbled and abandoned buildings were vandalized, looting became rife with tombstones even stolen from the graveyard. To arrest the rot, three caretakers were hired to police Bodie's vacant neighbourhoods but with only limited success, since

two of them quarrelled and refused to speak to each other when out on patrols. The solution finally came in 1962, when Brodie passed into the hands of the State of California and was made over into a State Historic Park. Rather than restore the town to its 1880s heyday, officials opted to preserve it in a 'state of arrested decay'. So today it stands as it was sixty years ago – a ruin of the old west from the time when *Rawhide* and *Gunsmoke* still aired on TV – and it is patched up from time to time to keep it looking just that way.

BELOW The old mining town of Bodie, California is now a ghost town, preserved in its decayed state.

FLAGSTAFF

MAINE, USA

45° 12' 53.4" N / 70° 21' 00.0" W

Few national flags are perhaps quite as fêted in their own land as that of the USA. 'Old Glory' or the Star-Spangled Banner is, after all, treated to a whole day in its honour – the annual National Flag Day on 14 June, an occasion, since its inauguration in 1916, marked by parades and such festivities as the eating of smoked meats and vegetables, and a holiday in some states. But it is also at the heart of the Pledge of Allegiance, the ritual performed daily in American public schools in which pupils, hands on hearts and eyes steadfast on the Stars and Stripes, repeat together a solemn oath 'to the flag' itself and only then 'to the republic for which it stands'.

With their roots in the primordial rags dipped in the blood of enemies conquered in battle and then raised high on sticks to signal victory, flags are, in essence, all about belonging. (We often speak of 'rallying round the flag' when a people come together against a perceived common threat from outside.) Serving as powerful visual emblems of a collective identity, their designs are often weighted with symbolic, ideological and political meanings. The Stars and Stripes is no exception. It was birthed in the fight for American independence from Britain and its distinctive red and white stripes can be traced back to a campaign by the self-styled Sons of Liberty against taxes imposed on the colony in the Stamp Act of 1765.

When the elm tree in Boston under which protests against the tax were held was cut down in an effort to dissuade such seditious gatherings, the Sons simply took to erecting a pole, up which they began hoisting a flag bearing nine red and white stripes (usually vertical) on it. The number of stripes corresponded to the nine colonies (Massachusetts, Connecticut, Rhode Island, New York, New Jersey, Pennsylvania, Delaware, Maryland and South Carolina) who objected to the new taxes. The flag, promptly outlawed by the British, was dubbed the 'Rebellious Stripe'. Variants of these striped liberty flags would serve as colours and standards during the American Revolution to come. Following independence, the first version of the Stars and Stripes was adopted for the new nation in 1777 – a flag incorporating thirteen horizontal red and white 'Rebellious Stripes' along with a constellation of thirteen white stars on a blue background (those numbers chosen to symbolize the thirteen original colonies).

History fails to record exactly what kind of flag Colonel Benedict Arnold chose to lead his revolutionary Continental Army forces under against the British. But we do know he certainly planted the odd flagpole during the period he battled for American autonomy. Arnold's exploits during the war for independence would make him a patriotic hero but he later turned traitor to the cause.

In December 1775, however, Arnold was still loyally fighting the good fight and was marching north to Quebec, where he and General Richard Montgomery were to lead what turned out to be a disastrous attempt to capture the British-occupied city and ferment support for the revolution in Canada. Montgomery was killed in the first assault and Arnold was shot in the leg, an injury that was to be exacerbated

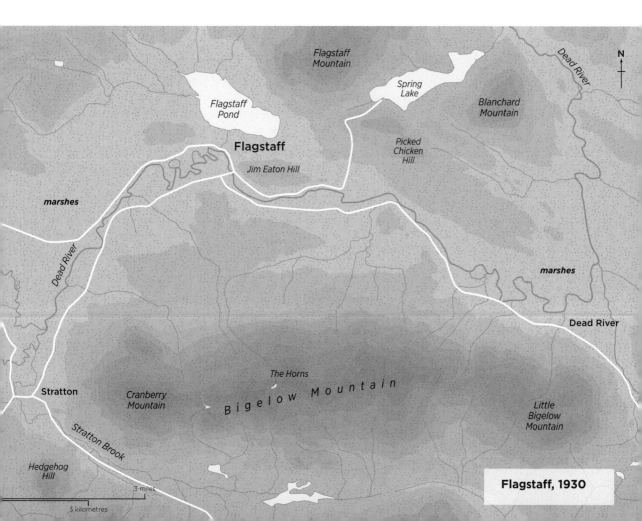

Flagstaff, 1930

by a subsequent wound in the same limb sustained during the Battle of Bemis Heights two years later.

Here, however, over 400 Continental Army men from a force of barely more than 1,000, lost their lives, while the British, who assailed the would-be intruders with a barrage of artillery and musket fire, suffered only minor casualties. The Battle of Quebec proved to be the first major defeat of the Revolutionary War for the Americans.

Of course, all this lay some weeks in the future when Arnold and his infantrymen were determinedly tracking their way across the wilderness of what is now Maine to reach the snow-laden Plains of Abraham across the border, and where they were to muster in preparation for the assault.

Flushed with the success of capturing the British garrison at Fort Ticonderoga in upstate New York just a few months earlier, we can imagine Arnold feeling pretty confident about their prospects and the decision to plant a flagstaff near their camp in what would become known as the Dead river floodplain undertaken in a spirit of enthusiastic revolutionary fervour.

Arnold's own enthusiasm for the revolution would wane and, feeling slighted by the promotion of men beneath him and accruing substantial debt as the Military Governor of Philadelphia, he chose to swap sides, selling out for a bounty to the British in 1780. But his

ABOVE: Flagstaff Lake seen from Bigelow Mountain.

flagstaff was discovered by an old trapper some years down the line. Once other settlers moved into the area in the early 1800s, attracted by the good soil, plentiful fresh water of the nearby lakes and rivers and rich sources of timber, maintaining the pole became a local tradition and the place that emerged was named after it.

In the 1840s, someone called Myles Standish established grist and sawmills at Flagstaff powered by a small nearby dam, and the town, along with the neighbouring village of Dead River Plantation, flourished and enjoyed a century of prosperity. But it would be another type of dam, erected at Long Falls on the Dead river by Walter Wyman's Central Maine Power company in 1949 to generate hydroelectricity, that would seal the fate of these two unfortunate settlements. Flagstaff and Dead River Plantation were to be drowned in the march to provide Maine at large with more electricity. The surrounding forest was cleared and bush cut and burned, and buildings such as the local school levelled, while others were left to be subsumed by the waters. According to a contemporary article in the Boston Globe on the eve of Independence Day in 1949, a two-day community farewell was begun at Flagstaff, with 300 residents returning to say their goodbyes

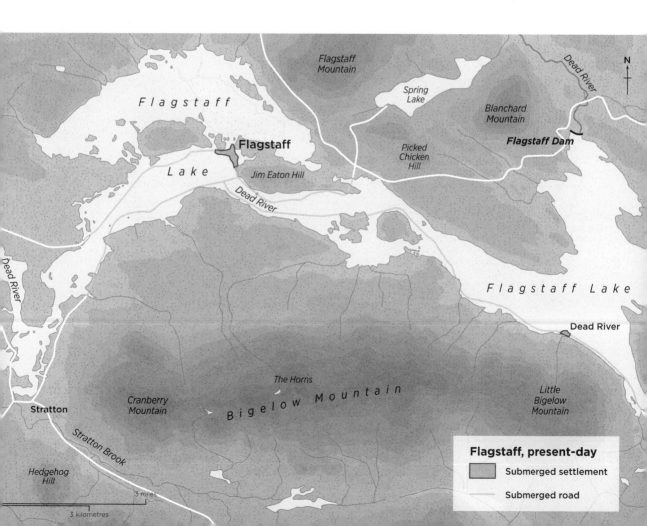

to their former home. Most of them, like the dearly departed interned in the Flagstaff and Dead River Cemeteries, had by then already been relocated to Eustis, a town close enough for community comfort but far enough away from the impeding deluge for safety. Although, at this point, some were still clinging on, stubbornly insisting they would not be moved out, their resistance, if spirited, was ultimately no more successful than Canute's attempts to hold back the waves.

Still, while old stories were swapped and well-burnished anecdotes of days gone by indulged in during this reunion of relatives, neighbours and old friends, discussion turned to the little matter of what to do about the flagstaff itself. After a few moments silence, the postmaster Evan Leavitt reportedly suggested leaving it where it was; the pole to stand as the last marker of Flagstaff itself as it perished beneath Maine's largest manmade lake. The plan seemingly adopted, the waters appear to have overwhelmed the pole when they rushed through the town the following spring. History is silent about what, if any, flag was flying on the day that they swamped Flagstaff. Though the right to desecrate the American flag has been legally upheld under the freedom of speech clause in the First Amendment to the United States Constitution, the prospect of losing a Star Spangled Banner, the standard of the Republic, as well as the whole town, might just have been too much for anyone to bear.

BELOW Main Street of Flagstaff before the flooding.

ABOVE Flagstaff's remaining
buildings being flooded in 1950.

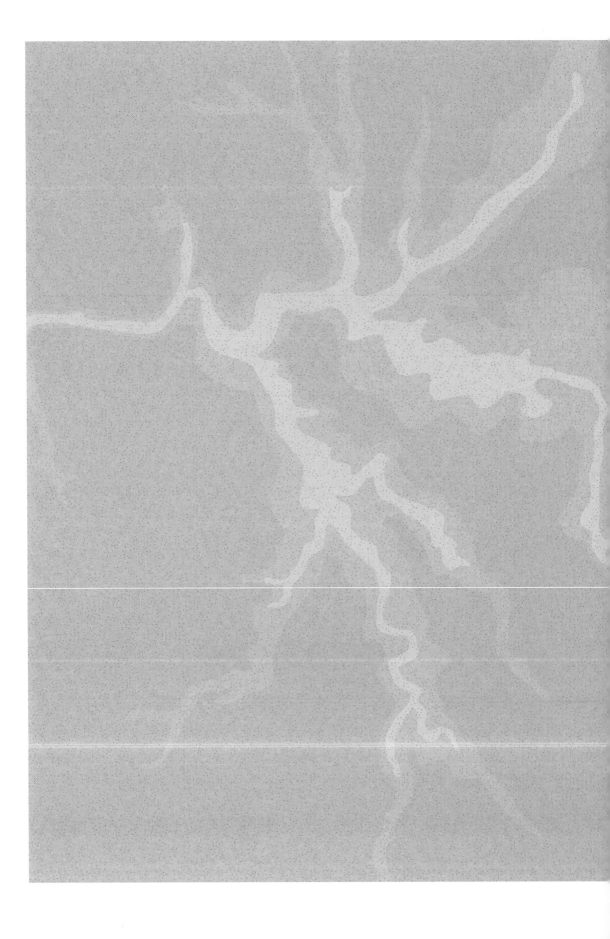

SHRINKING PLACES

RIVER DANUBE

EUROPE

48° 13′ 18.1″ N / 16° 24′ 52.3″ E

In his Cosmographia, the sixteenth-century German cartographer and cosmographer Sebastian Münster would claim that the River Danube began life as a drainage channel from the times of Noah and the biblical flood. But its waters, also said to have been sailed by the Golden Fleece-seeking Jason and the Argonauts of Greek myth and hailed as 'the greatest of all the rivers which we know' by the 'Father of History' Herodotus, have run their current course, more or less, for close to three million years. As such, the river has provided a backdrop to the monumental shifts in European history, a witness equally to the arrival of the earliest Mesolithic human society and the birth and expansion of the European Union, as well as the rise and fall of the Macedonian, Roman, Habsburg and Ottoman empires, Nazi Germany and the Soviet Union. While the lands around it have changed shapes and names, the Danube has appeared an almost constant, if actually still much shifting, presence on charts of the continent since the earliest days of mapmaking.

The Danube stretches from its source in the Black Forest in southern Germany to Sulina, the easternmost point of Romania, where the land promptly gives way to sand and the lapping waves of the Black Sea. Unique among the major European rivers for travelling west to east rather than north to south, its 1,777-mile (2,850-km) course currently crosses ten countries – Germany, Austria, Slovakia, Hungary, Croatia, Serbia, Bulgaria, Romania, Moldova and the Ukraine. Serving for centuries as a bridge between Europe and Asia, the Danube has equally acted as a barrier both between the east and west and the north and south. The river still separates present-day Slovakia and Hungary and helps define Romania's borders with Serbia, the Ukraine and Bulgaria.

N

Viennese Danube, *c.* 1849

River course

Marshland

Jedlesee

Leopoldau

Floridsdorf

Donaufeld

Kagran

Hirschstetten

Stadlau

Aspern

Rossau

V I E N N A

old city walls

Leopoldstadt

aimgrube

Landstrasse

Favoriten

Donaukanal (Danube Canal)

0   2000 yards

0   2000 metres

In classical times Alexander the Great opted to use the Danube –
or the Ister, as the ancient Greeks knew it – to determine the upper
limits of his empire. The Romans, similarly having founded Vindobona
(Vienna) as a military stronghold at a favourable site on its banks,
stationed troops along the length of the river to defend their territories
from marauding northern hoards. More recently though and during
the Cold War, when 'an iron curtain' fell across Europe separating the
communist countries of the Soviet Union in the east from those of the
capitalist west, the Danube, like the city of Berlin, was divided, with
a kind of liquid roadblock operating between Vienna and Bratislava
and splicing the river into western and eastern halves. After the fall of
the Soviet Union and the end of the Balkan Wars, shipping remained
stalled at Novi Sad, the Serbian city whose Freedom Bridge over the
Danube was bombed by Nato in 1999.

Today, and thanks to European Union funding, the whole length
of the river is once again navigable. But the eastern end of the Danube
remains heavily at risk from a future ecological disaster. Unprotected
pools of heavy metals and toxic sludge have been identified in defunct
plants and reservoirs near the river in Hungary, Serbia and Romania.
The legacy of heavy industries such as bauxite and uranium mining,
promoted by the regimes of the Soviet bloc, they threaten to leak into
its waterway with potentially devastating consequences for the river
basin as a whole.

ABOVE: 1894 engraving of the
opening of the new navigation
canal at the mouth of the Danube
in Sulina, Romania.

N

Jedlesee

Leopoldau

New Danube

Floridsdorf

Donaufeld

Kagran

Alte Donau (Old Danube)

Brigittenau

Hirschstetten

Zwischenbrücken

D A N U B E

Rossau

Stadlau

Leopoldstadt

Aspern

V I E N N A

Laimgrube

Landstrasse

New Danube

Favoriten

Donaukanal (Danube Canal)

Viennese Danube, present-day

River course

0   2000 yards

0   2000 metres

Always a working river, the Danube as it stands is fundamentally a product of modern industrialization, its present form shaped by the wharves, docks and shipyards assembled along its banks, themselves heavily embanked and canalized, and the bridges thrown up over it. This process was begun in earnest in the 1870s, when the French construction company Castor, Couvreux et Hersent, who had worked on the Suez Canal, were hired to re-route a meandering 8-mile (12-km) long stretch of the river at Vienna into a new straight riverbed, the first of a series of such 'improvements' undertaken along its course in the late nineteenth century, and throughout the twentieth century. The Danube we have now has lost some 80 per cent of its original flood plain, and only 30 per cent of it is free-flowing. As an elderly Heinrich Heine once admonished a young Karl Marx to remember, 'the difference between water and a river is that the latter has a memory, a past, a history'. If the Danube has that in spades, it is up to us to ensure it also has a healthy future too.

BELOW: The industrial banks of the Danube in Linz, Austria at sunset.

THE DEAD SEA

JORDAN/ISRAEL

31° 29' 33.2" N / 35° 28' 40.3" E

In Arabic it is known as Bahr el-Lut, the Sea of Lot; in Hebrew and to the Jewish community it remains Yam Ha-Melah, the Salt Sea, a name that it has borne since the biblical era and that first appears in the Book of Genesis. In Jewish history it was also referred to as the East Sea, a name that both distinguished it from the Mediterranean and linguistically in Hebrew carries connotations with the idea of the past. By tradition more than scripture it is, in both cultures, closely associated with the destruction of the four of five cities of the plain, Sodom, Gomorrah, Admah and Zeboiim (Tso'ar or Zoar was spared) – an event that most probably has some basis in an ancient geological catastrophe in the region. Yet it wasn't until the Romans, following the Greeks, who were enchanted by its peculiar qualities, dubbed it *Mare Mortuum* – the Dead Sea – that any sense of lifelessness attached itself to this expanse of saline-heavy water that lies between contemporary Israel and Jordan.

Worse, in a sense, was to come. Christian pilgrims in the Middle Ages, for whom it became a stopping off point between Mount Sinai and Jerusalem, called it the Devil's Sea and believed all manner of grotesque creatures lurked below its surface and that its waters gave off fetid and noxious vapours. The Stinking Lake was another name that attached itself to the sea, in acknowledgement of the sulphurous odours that certainly emanated, and continue to emanate, from it. But it is only within the last fifty years or so that the Dead Sea can truly be said to have entered what could well be its terminal phase.

If admittedly presenting a rather barren prospect, with the rocky Moab mountains and Judean Desert framing the scene at either side, the Dead Sea basin has been continuously occupied since prehistoric times, with the cities of Jericho to its north and Tso'ar (Zoar) to the south among its most historic settlements. The sea itself dates back to the same shift in

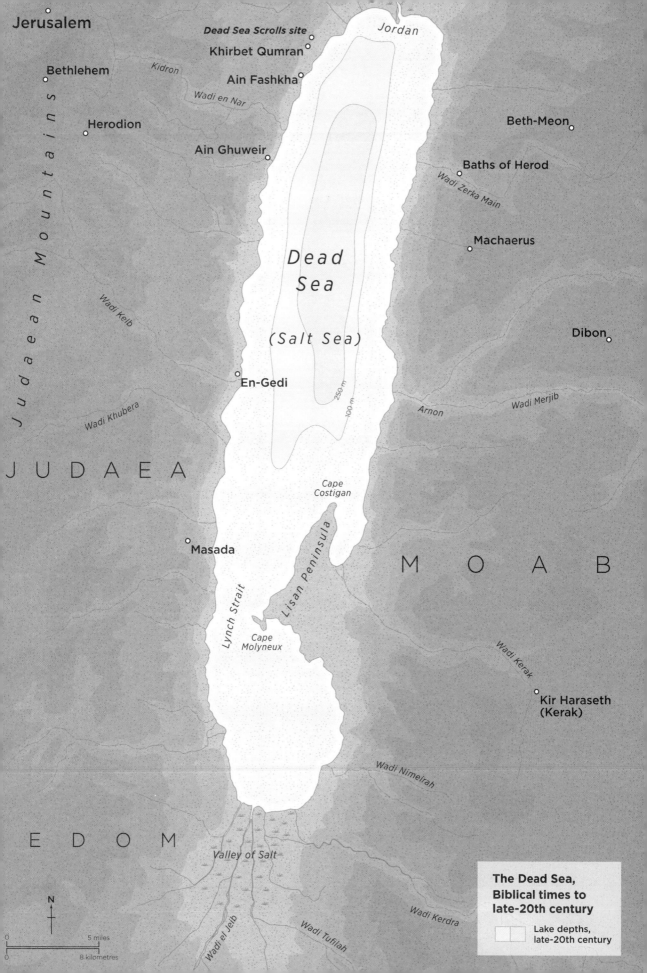

Jerusalem

Bethlehem

Herodion

Judaean Mountains

Kidron

Wadi en Nar

Ain Ghuweir

Wadi Kelb

Wadi Khubera

J U D A E A

En-Gedi

Masada

Lynch Strait

*Cape
Molyneux*

E D O M

Valley of Salt

N

0 ____ 5 miles
0 ____ 8 kilometres

Dead Sea Scrolls site
Khirbet Qumran

Ain Fashkha

Jordan

Dead
Sea

(Salt Sea)

250 m

100 m

Cape
Costigan

Lisan Peninsula

Beth-Meon

Baths of Herod

Wadi Zerka Main

Machaerus

Dibon

Arnon   *Wadi Merjib*

M O A B

Wadi Kerak

Kir Haraseth
(Kerak)

Wadi Nimeirah

Wadi el Jeib   *Wadi Tufilah*   *Wadi Kerdra*

**The Dead Sea,
Biblical times to
late-20th century**

Lake depths,
late-20th century

tectonic plates several million years ago that produced the Great Rift Valley, which runs from south-west Asia to east Africa and in which the sea lies. Probably once part of an even older lake that reached to the Sea of Galilee, the Dead Sea sits at the lowest place on earth at some 427m (1,400ft) below sea level. The next lowest places, by comparison, and clocking in at a mere minus 152m (500ft), are Lake Assal in Djibouti or the Turfan Depression in China. In the Western Hemisphere, only Death Valley in California at 85m (280ft) below sea level, comes anywhere near. Up to seven times more salty than other oceans, the Dead Sea is sustained by the flow of water from the River Jordan at its northern end and the rivers and streams from the surrounding mountains. Evaporation and the rich local rock salt deposits explain its hyper-salinity, with its waters composed of something like 33 per cent salt. Utah's Great Salt Lake in America, meanwhile, only manages a 27 per cent rating at best.

Since the 1960s and 70s, however, when Israel, Jordan and Syria began diverting water from the Upper Jordan and Yarmouk rivers, the lower Jordan's main tributary, to feed the demand for water for agriculture and in their expanding towns and cities, the Dead Sea has declined and quite alarmingly so. Once 50 miles (80km) long, it currently stretches for barely 30 miles (48km) and its water levels are falling at a rate of 1m (3ft) a year.

What is at risk is not just a unique natural phenomenon that has defined an entire area for more than two millennia – a place that abounds with sites sacred to Jews, Christians and Muslims – but the whole of the surrounding ecosystem. The retreat of the sea has produced a profusion of sink holes, all threatening to undermine the neighbouring roads and properties, among them the numerous hotels that cater to tourists and pilgrims who seek to bathe in the Dead Sea's supposedly restorative brine. Only drastic action to replenish its waters will, in the end, avert something close to a catastrophe in the coming decades.

FOLLOWING PAGE: Sink holes near the Dead Sea in Ein Gedi, Israel, 2012.

BELOW: The Dead Sea is at risk from rapidly receding water levels.

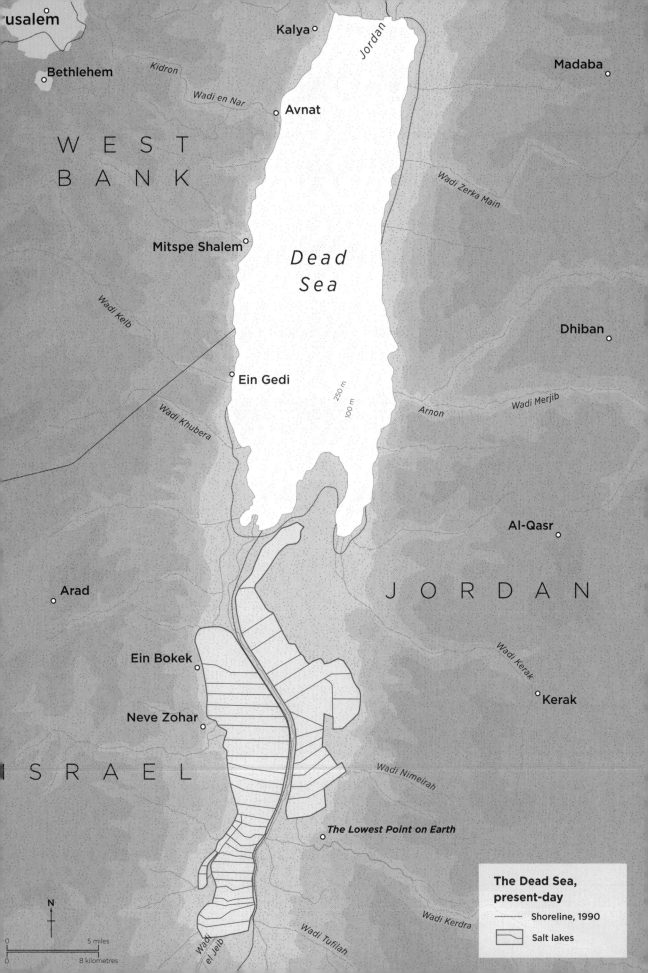

usalem

Bethlehem

Kalya

Madaba

Kidron

Wadi en Nar

Avnat

W E S T

B A N K

Wadi Zerka Main

Mitspe Shalem

*Dead
Sea*

Wadi Kelb

Dhiban

250 m

100 m

Ein Gedi

Wadi Khubera

Arnon

Wadi Merjib

Al-Qasr

Arad

J O R D A N

Wadi Kerak

Ein Bokek

Kerak

Neve Zohar

Wadi Nimeirah

I S R A E L

The Lowest Point on Earth

N

5 miles

8 kilometres

*Wadi
el Jeib*

Wadi Tufilah

Wadi Kerdra

**The Dead Sea,
present-day**

.... Shoreline, 1990

Salt lakes

SLIMS RIVER

YUKON, CANADA

60° 54' 16.6" N / 138° 38' 06.9" W

While the phrase 'river piracy' perhaps conjures up images of boat-borne marauders sailing into estuaries and rivers to loot and plunder, the term has quite a specific meaning for geomorphologists. These are the scientists who study the changes in the Earth's surface and substrata, along with the floors of the oceans and inland riverbeds. For them 'river piracy' refers to the phenomenon when the headwaters from one river are, in effect, stolen by another. Evidence of this had always been discerned in the geological record, with such changes from thousands or millions of years ago written, quite literally, in stone. Yet in 2016, geomorphologists found themselves in the remarkable position of being able to observe an instance of river piracy first hand, when the Slims river in Canada disappeared in just four days.

The effects on the local landscape have been profound. Dall sheep nibble vegetation where water once flowed. Fish have been displaced, and in their stead only an exposed and dusty bed of mud and sedimentary rock where until very recently they might have swum and spawned. The shoreline communities of Burwash Landing and Destruction Bay no longer have a river to complete the scene; any boats or canoes now seem somewhat surplus to requirements. If the abruptness of this unforeseen event was shocking, what its occurrence might ultimately foretell for this region, and the environment globally, was even more so.

For at least 300 years, the Slims River had been sustained by the Kaskawulsh glacier in the St Elias Mountain valley of Canada's Yukon territory, an area famed for the Klondike Gold Rush of the 1890s and the chilly grandeur of its sparsely populated terrain of mountain ranges, lakes, tundra and boreal forests. Water from the glacier's melting ice sheets kept the Slims on a north-easterly course, its streams

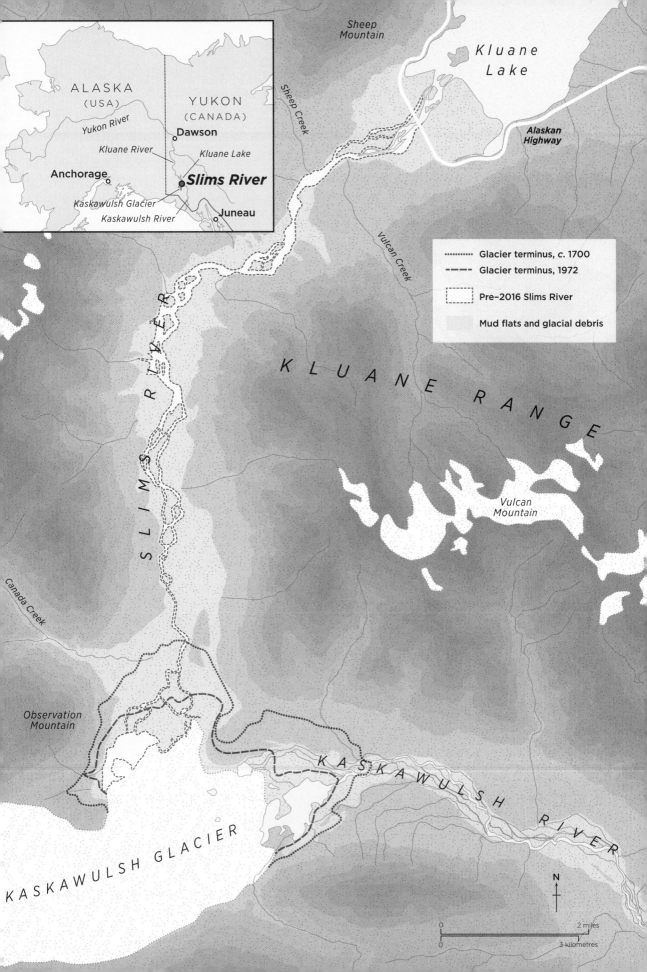

Sheep
Mountain

*Kluane
Lake*

Sheep Creek

**Alaskan
Highway**

ALASKA
(USA)

YUKON
(CANADA)

Yukon River

Dawson

Kluane River

Kluane Lake

Anchorage

Slims River

Kaskawulsh Glacier

Kaskawulsh River

Juneau

Vulcan Creek

Glacier terminus, *c.* 1700

Glacier terminus, 1972

Pre–2016 Slims River

Mud flats and glacial debris

S L I M S   R I V E R

K L U A N E   R A N G E

*Vulcan
Mountain*

Canada Creek

*Observation
Mountain*

K A S K A W U L S H   R I V E R

KASKAWULSH GLACIER

N

0   2 miles

0   3 kilometres

feeding the Kluane Lake and flowing on into the Bering Sea. But in just a few days in the spring of 2016, the glacier, which is one of Canada's largest, melted faster and retreated further than ever before. Its retreat altered the gradient of the meltwaters, diverting their course south to nourish the nearby Kaskawulsh river into the Gulf of Alaska, and away from the Slims. Before that the glacier had supplied water equally to both rivers, as it sat on the border between their two drainage basins, but in its new shrunken form, that balance shifted demonstrably with the result that the Slims was starved at source while the Kaskawulsh gushed on, reinvigorated with the excess.

The chances of the Slims river ever returning to its former glory are unlikely. Only an equally sudden glacial advance could potentially restore the course of the meltwater and, given current predictions for rising rather than falling temperatures in this part of North America, that doesn't seem destined to happen any time soon. Further retreats look set to bring equally unpredictable changes to the Yukon's topography, with inevitable consequences for the life and livelihoods of all its residents: human, animal, avian, aquatic and vegetable.

OPPOSITE: The Slims River flowing into Kluane Lake.

BELOW: A view of Kluane Lake and glacial deposits of the Slims River on the edge of Kluane National Park.

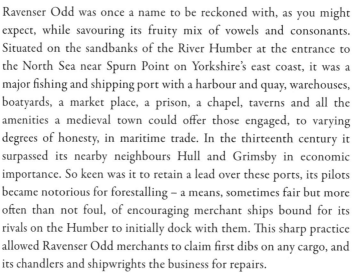

SKIPSEA

YORKSHIRE, UK

53° 58′ 45.1″ N / 0° 11′ 60.0″ W

Ravenser Odd was once a name to be reckoned with, as you might expect, while savouring its fruity mix of vowels and consonants. Situated on the sandbanks of the River Humber at the entrance to the North Sea near Spurn Point on Yorkshire's east coast, it was a major fishing and shipping port with a harbour and quay, warehouses, boatyards, a market place, a prison, a chapel, taverns and all the amenities a medieval town could offer those engaged, to varying degrees of honesty, in maritime trade. In the thirteenth century it surpassed its nearby neighbours Hull and Grimsby in economic importance. So keen was it to retain a lead over these ports, its pilots became notorious for forestalling – a means, sometimes fair but more often than not foul, of encouraging merchant ships bound for its rivals on the Humber to initially dock with them. This sharp practice allowed Ravenser Odd merchants to claim first dibs on any cargo, and its chandlers and shipwrights the business for repairs.

When the story of this town later came to be told, some would see divine retribution in its eventual fate; the Lord appearing to take such a dim view of Ravenser Odd's nautical finagling that he commanded the sea to wipe it off the earth. God sanctioned or not, in the 1340s the sandbanks on which it stood shifted and many of the houses were swept away. By 1355 more than two thirds of the town lay under water and the majority of its inhabitants had abandoned it. Seven years later, a terrible storm known (with almost pitiful literalism) as the Great Drowning of Men raged across the east coast and carried what little else remained of Ravenser Odd into the sea.

Over twenty other towns and villages standing along this stretch of east Yorkshire – the Holderness coast that runs from Flamborough down to Spurn Point – have fallen into the North Sea since the Middle

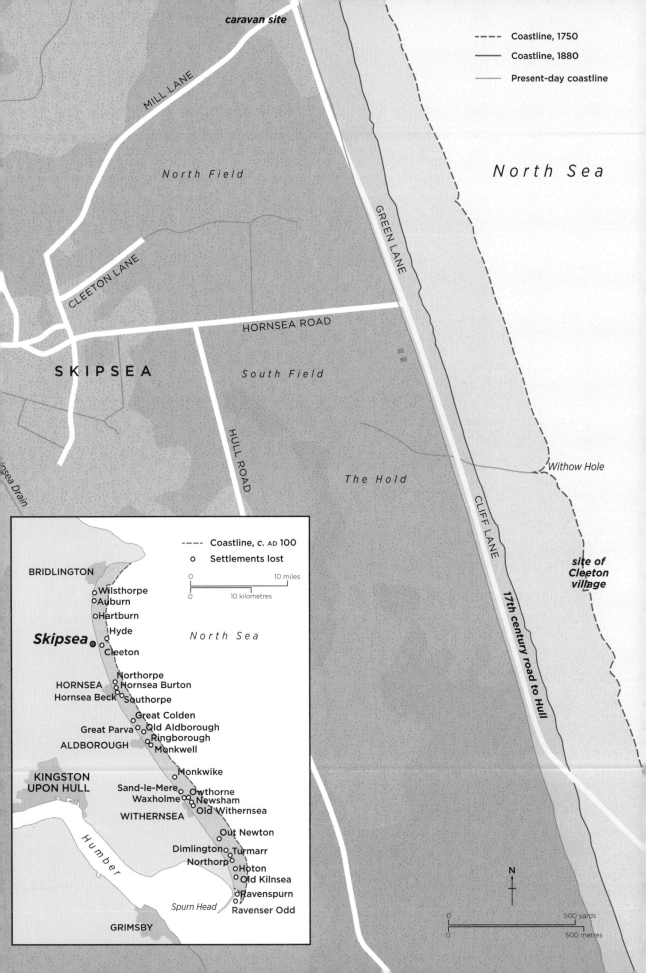

caravan site

MILL LANE

North Field

CLEETON LANE

GREEN LANE

HORNSEA ROAD

SKIPSEA

South Field

HULL ROAD

The Hold

CLIFF LANE

Withow Hole

site of Cleeton village

17th century road to Hull

North Sea

- - - - Coastline, 1750
———— Coastline, 1880
———— Present-day coastline

nsea Drain

N

| 0 | | | 500 yards |
| 0 | | | 500 metres |

BRIDLINGTON

- - - Coastline, *c.* AD 100
○ Settlements lost

| 0 | | 10 miles |
| 0 | | 10 kilometres |

o Wilsthorpe
o Auburn
o Hartburn
Hyde

Skipsea ●
o Cleeton

North Sea

Northorpe
HORNSEA o Hornsea Burton
Hornsea Beck o Southorpe
Great Colden
Great Parva o Old Aldborough
Ringborough
ALDBOROUGH Monkwell

Monkwike

KINGSTON UPON HULL

Sand-le-Mere o Owthorne
Waxholme o Newsham
WITHERNSEA Old Withernsea

Out Newton

Dimlington o Turmarr
Northorp
o Hoton
o Old Kilnsea
o Ravenspurn
Spurn Head Ravenser Odd

Humber

GRIMSBY

Ages. Such has been the pace of coastal erosion in this part of England that some now lie 3½ miles (6km) off shore. In a survey of these departed settlements published in the Yorkshire Archaeological Journal in 1952, the local historian M.W. Beresford, succinctly gave the single word 'drowned' as the explanation for the loss of Cleeton, a one-time south easterly neighbour to Skipsea. And unless urgent action is taken, the seaside settlement of Skipsea, with its caravan parks, clifftop chalets and bungalows, looks set to follow Cleeton, just as Cleeton followed Hyde, the port just to the north of it lost over six centuries ago.

Turn the clocks back even further, though, to the age of Roman Britain and the land where Skipsea stands so precariously today, was nearly an hour or more's walk from the sea. The settlement, which grew up around the castle and manor established in Norman times, would only become properly coastal in around 1600. From the Old Norse, skip, for a ship, and saer, for a lake, its name derived from a mere whose waters once ran through a series of navigable channels out into the River Hull. This was subsequently drained, leaving an expanse of fertile silt that made good farmland. Lingering traces of the area's formerly extensive agricultural activity can be spied in the dilapidated outbuildings, ruined shacks and rusting machinery on the gone-to-seed plots that dot the areas between Ulrome and Skipsea.

Since the 1930s, when holiday chalets were built on the cliffs at Southwick Farm, Skipsea has been a coastal destination, providing a quieter and more modest offering for seekers of fresh air, briny water and other distractions than the region's main resorts at Hornsea

and Withernsea. Visitors, who arrived in greater numbers with the erection of caravan parks in the 1950s and 60s, have been attracted by the austere beauty of the landscape here, where shallow, grassy flatlands abruptly end in crumbly russet-brown cliffs that reach down to sandy beaches and the ever-lapping waves of the North Sea. But composed of clay left over from the glaciers that retreated at the end of the last ice age and when the North Sea retained the quality of a muddy swamp fed by the Rhine and the Humber, this soft boulder coastline has been eroding almost from the moment of its creation. Today it is officially Europe's fastest-eroding coast. Current rates put retreat between Skipsea and Spurn Point at 1.5–2m (5–6½ft) a year, but in more recent times there have been moments of far more rapid and violent collapse with as much as 20m (65ft) of cliff disappearing on one or two occasions overnight.

Cliff collapses have rendered what was once the main road further south into the Sand-Le-Mere holiday park at Tunstall out of bounds while other road closures due to erosion mean that the residents of Green Lane in Skipsea can only access their properties from the rear. Some residents blame the construction of certain sea defences along the coast at Mappleton, Withernsea and Easington for exacerbating the situation by channelling waters in their direction. But while schemes are in place to improve defences as well as accepting a degree of 'sustainable' decline, with the sea already predicted to rise by a metre (3ft) in the next hundred years, Skipsea's continued existence is far from assured.

BELOW: The coastal erosion of the cliffs at Skipsea.

THE EVERGLADES

FLORIDA, USA

25° 16' 50.3" N / 80° 53' 58.1" W

Throughout Donald Trump's 2016 election campaign, the former reality television star and property mogul repeatedly promised to 'drain the swamp' if he were elected to the presidency. The phrase, which he reiterated on twitter in block capitals and with an exclamation mark ('DRAIN THE SWAMP!') was eagerly adopted by his supporters who took to chanting it at his rallies. Trump's swamp was, nevertheless, a purely metaphorical one. It apparently referred to what he judged as the undue influence of lobbyists in government and echoed Ronald Reagan's similar comments about reducing Washington's so-called 'bureaucracy'. Yet back at the turn of the last century one politician, the Democrat Napoleon Bonaparte Broward, was elected to office on a far less figurative version of the same slogan. And the state to which Broward was elected governor was Florida, where, as it happens, Mar-a-Lago, Trump's self-styled 'winter White House' at Palm Beach, is also located.

Born on the family plantation in Duval County in 1857, Broward was the offspring of Florida's slave-owning antebellum elite. One of the few things he arguably did inherit from his forebears was some pretty odious views on race. Still, the Browards, loyal supporters of the Confederacy, were to see their farms sacked and their slaves liberated by Union troops during the Civil War. Forced to sell off most of what was left in its aftermath, the clan struggled ever after to remain financially solvent. With school fees beyond the family's depleted circumstances, the young Napoleon remained at home to plant potatoes and sugar cane in the fields, crops that, as he later recalled, not infrequently failed.

Further misery was added at the age of 12 when Broward was orphaned. In quick succession, his mother, a long-term invalid,

committed suicide and then his father, a former captain in the Confederate army who'd taken to drink, caught pneumonia and died, shortly after conducting an all-night vigil at his late wife's graveside. Subsequent misfortunes to befall Broward would be the death of his own first wife through childbirth, and their young daughter shortly afterwards. But at this juncture and encumbered with a plot of near worthless farmland with poor prospects, Broward turned to tending orange groves and rafting logs to earn a buck, until finally finding his vocation as a deckhand on a steamboat on the St Johns river.

By the age of 30, Broward possessed a tug of his own and was a prosperous entrepreneur, with an ever-expanding range of business interests in salvage, shipbuilding, lumber, dredging and phosphate mining. A formidable physical presence, standing 1.9m (6ft 2in) tall and always sporting an immaculately groomed, if soup-disturbingly bushy, walrus moustache, Broward was well liked for his honest dealing and his down-home folksy persona and un-spun speech. Respected for refusing to sell liquor on his riverboats, he used his first public appointment, as sheriff of Jacksonville, to lead crusades against corruption, gambling and such unseemly public sporting contests as boxing matches. Having come to national prominence for using his sea tug, The Three Friends, to run arms to American-backed, anti-Spanish rebels in Cuba during the Spanish–American War of 1898, Broward set his sights on the governorship of his home state in 1904.

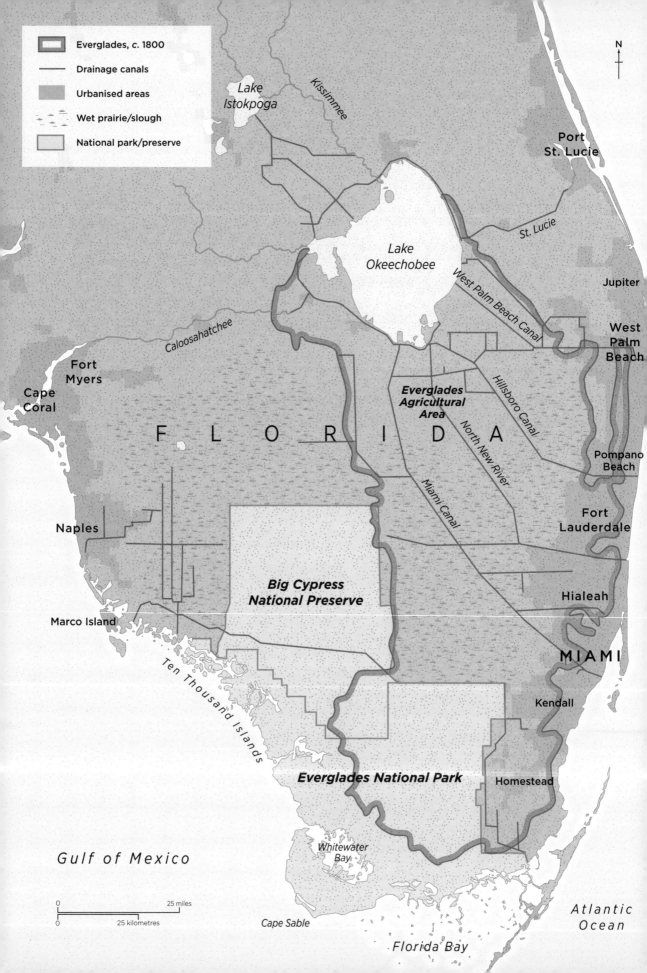

Everglades, _c._ 1800

Drainage canals

Urbanised areas

Wet prairie/slough

National park/preserve

N

Lake
Istokpoga

Kissimmee

Port
St. Lucie

Lake
Okeechobee

St. Lucie

Jupiter

Caloosahatchee

West Palm Beach Canal

West
Palm
Beach

Fort
Myers

Cape
Coral

**Everglades
Agricultural
Area**

Hillsboro Canal

Pompano
Beach

F L O R I D A

North New River

Miami Canal

Fort
Lauderdale

Naples

Hialeah

**Big Cypress
National Preserve**

Marco Island

MIAMI

Kendall

Ten Thousand Islands

Everglades National Park

Homestead

_Whitewater
Bay_

Gulf of Mexico

_Atlantic
Ocean_

0   25 miles

0   25 kilometres

Cape Sable

Florida Bay

Of all the electoral promises that ensured his eventual victory, none did more for his prospects among the ordinary voters he courted, than Broward's commitment to wring every last drop of water out of that 'pestilence-ridden swamp' and create an 'Empire of the Everglades'.

Once entirely underwater, Florida's Everglades, the massive wetlands affectionately known as 'the river of grass', developed over the centuries into a series of rain- and river-fed tidal marshes, mangrove swamps, fens and lakes, and hardwood rich uplands. Covering almost 12,140 square kilometres (3,000,000 acres) and running from just south of the modern city of Orlando through Lake Okeechobee down to the southern tip of the peninsula, the Everglades were first comprehensively surveyed by the US Secretary of War and future (and sole) President of the Confederate States, Jefferson Davis, with the 'Davis Map' published in 1856.

A scheme to drain parts of the Everglades had, in fact, already been initiated by Broward's predecessor William Sherman Jennings. But Broward was a man on a mission. In response to those who doubted the feasibility of his stated dream of installing a new class of homesteaders on Florida's most sodden expanses, he flatly retorted: 'Yes, the Everglades is a swamp; so was Chicago sixty years ago.'

Inland drainage operations would commence in 1906. Within four years Broward would be dead, aged just 51, and having only recently secured election to the US senate. But what he had set in motion was ultimately to result in the shrinkage of the Everglades to less than half their original size. By 1922, the sheer number of adverts for new land for sale in Florida carried by the *Miami Herald* would make it the heaviest newspaper per paper weight in the USA.

The rapid urbanization and industrial expansion of southern Florida, with new highways joining the eventual 1,800 miles (2,900km) of canals and dams crisscrossing the state, was largely seen as a sign of progress and a harbinger of affluence. The initial hardy yeomen, would-be smallholders, scientific agriculturalists, canny speculators and the all-out carpetbaggers of dubious intent, were in time followed by Fordian vegetable growers and fruit canners, real-estate developers, theme-park designers, sun-seeking tourists and retirees. But by 1920s a few voices already started to be raised about the depletion of the wetlands.

In 1928, the landscape architect and gardener Ernest F. Coe, who had settled in Coconut Grove, Miami, three years earlier and become enraptured by the abundance of wildlife in the Everglades, began arguing for part of it to be preserved as a national park. Overcoming opposition from landowners and the indifference of state officials who failed to see its worth to the wider community, his proposal was at last adopted by President Roosevelt who signed the Everglades National Park act in 1934, though it would take another thirteen years before all the compensation claims and the precise parameters of the park to be agreed.

Dedicated by President Truman in 1947, who noted that while there were 'no lofty peaks seeking the sky' or 'mighty glaciers or rushing streams', there was tranquility 'in its quiet beauty', and that the land here served 'not as the source of water, but as the last receiver of it', the Everglades National Park was to measure 6,000 square kilometres (1.5 million acres) in total. It was the first national park in America to be established on the basis of what were described as its 'biological wonders'. But within twenty years of its founding, such indigenous beauties as the Florida panther, the snail kite and the Cape Sable seaside sparrow had already been added to the federal government's endangered-species list.

Worse still, they would soon be joined by the likes of the American crocodile whose numbers in the Florida Bay area were calculated in the mid-1970s to have dwindled to a meagre 200 specimens. If conservation was finally to become a major political issue in the ensuing decades, and successive administrations committed to restoring the Everglades to a more natural state, they presently continue to languish in a critical, if not near terminal, condition. As such, they mirror the vulnerability of much of the state as a whole, which has experienced an increase in the number and strength of hurricanes and more persistent inland flooding in recent years. With the sea predicted to rise by 1.5m (5ft) by the end of this century, the whole of the city of Miami and up to a million homes in the metropolitan areas could disappear beneath the waves.

The encroachment of saltwater at the Everglades, which also threatens to swamp it entirely, has already caused the retreat of the marshes. The mangroves, those areas of coastal vegetation that grow in the brackish water, which also serve as habitats for an array of different creatures, have been heading further and further inland, retreating at a rate of 30m (100ft) per year on what has been called a 'death march' to escape the swelling ocean. The Everglades' fragile ecosystem has been under attack from fertilizers used in agriculture that decades ago infiltrated its waters, along with a phalanx of invasive non-indigenous plants and animals. Among the most deadly has been the Melaleuca. A fast-growing tree from Australia, the Melaleuca was introduced into southern Florida in the early 1900s and planted en masse on the strength of its ability to help dry out swampland. What it also did was to spread like wildfire, the thickets monopolizing the sawgrass marshes and wet prairies, and choking the life out of native plants.

Just as damaging has been the Brazilian pepper. A South American ornamental shrub almost as sharp-elbowed as its Australian forerunner, it was first imported into North America in the 1950s and largely to add a touch of exotic international glamour to suburban gardens – its appeal to post-war homemakers not unlike, say, Bossa Nova music of the same period. A similar story can be told of the Burmese pythons in the Everglades, which were most likely kept as domestic pets and either escaped from, or were abandoned by, their negligent owners. Since the late 1980s the pythons have bred successfully becoming a significant predator of the birds, young mammals and crocodiles around the rivers, marshes and lakes, and upending a food chain that for some of its most threatened species was already desperately precarious. As it stands, the Everglades teeter on the brink of extinction – only drastic action and perhaps a politician brave enough to stand up for swamps rather than wishing to drain them, will have any hope of saving them.

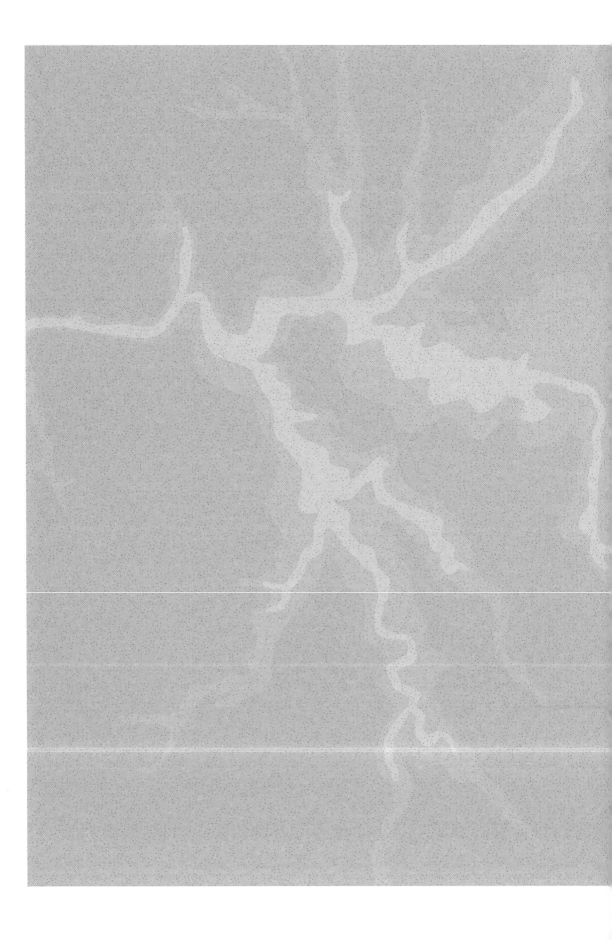

THREATENED WORLDS

GLACIER NATIONAL PARK

MONTANA, USA

48° 44' 48.7" N / 113° 47' 14.4" W

It was in 1864, and in the midst of the American Civil War, that President Abraham Lincoln signed the Yosemite Grant Act. This was the first piece of US Government legislation to set aside a scenic wilderness (Yosemite, California) for public use and preservation and, if a while coming, paved the way for the establishment of America's subsequent national parks. In that same year, and as a response to southern states seceding in the years prior to that, the Montana Territory was welcomed into the Union, joining such other western districts as Nevada, Arizona and Idaho – though it would have to wait until 1886 for full statehood. But what a state it would be. Extending from the Rockies in the west to the rolling Great Plains of the east and with Yellowstone National Park to the south, its landscape is one of contrasts, ranging from high snow-capped mountains, deep valleys, green forests and freshwater lakes to flat expanses of shortgrass prairies, fields of yellow grain and dusty brown fallow lands.

Along its border with Canada in the northwestern part of the state and nestled in the Rocky Mountains, is a narrow valley, crested with ice, of extraordinarily rugged beauty. Known to the Blackfeet tribe of Native Americans as 'the backbone of the world', in the 1890s it was dubbed the 'crown of the continent' by the journalist George Grinnell. It was Grinnell who, in extolling the natural glories of the area in print, helped open the eyes of the world at large to their wonders. He was also the first person to suggest that part of this area should become a national park, an idea given political heft by the support of Montana Congressman Charles N. Pray. The Glacier National Park was finally born on 11 May 1910 and in 1932 it would also become the first 'international peace park', when it was officially twinned with Canada's Waterton Lakes National Park just over the border.

ABOVE Grinnell Glacier in 2016. Between 1966 and 2015 it had diminished by 45 per cent.

Alone, the Glacier National Park covers more than a million acres, or 1,600 square miles (4,144 square kilometres). It contains two mountain ranges, including six peaks that rise over 3,000m (10,000ft), 130 lakes and 1,000 different varieties of plant life, and 100 animal species, among them grizzly bears, mountain goats, pygmy shrews, elk and bighorn sheep. As its name suggests, however, glaciers are, or perhaps more accurately were, one of the park's most remarkable features.

Around 2.6 million years ago in the Pleistocene Epoch, huge parts of the earth were covered by glaciers, the chilling conditions of this, the last ice age, were to cause sea levels in the Northern Hemisphere to drop by over 90m (300ft). Parts of where Montana and the Rocky Mountains are today would have been covered in ice up to a mile (1.6km) deep. The great thaw, however, began around 12,000 years ago, and the dynamic landscape of this region is the result of melting ice flows shifting and exposing sedimentary rock.

The remaining glaciers of the park are calculated to be about 7,000 years old and, like all glaciers are masses of ice, snow, water and rock sediment formed when the seasonal accumulation of ice and snow in winter exceeds spring and summer melting. Research into the park's history has revealed that there were 150 glaciers in 1850. At present there are 37, of which only 25 are described as active, and during the last century these ice formations have lost 85 per cent of their size.

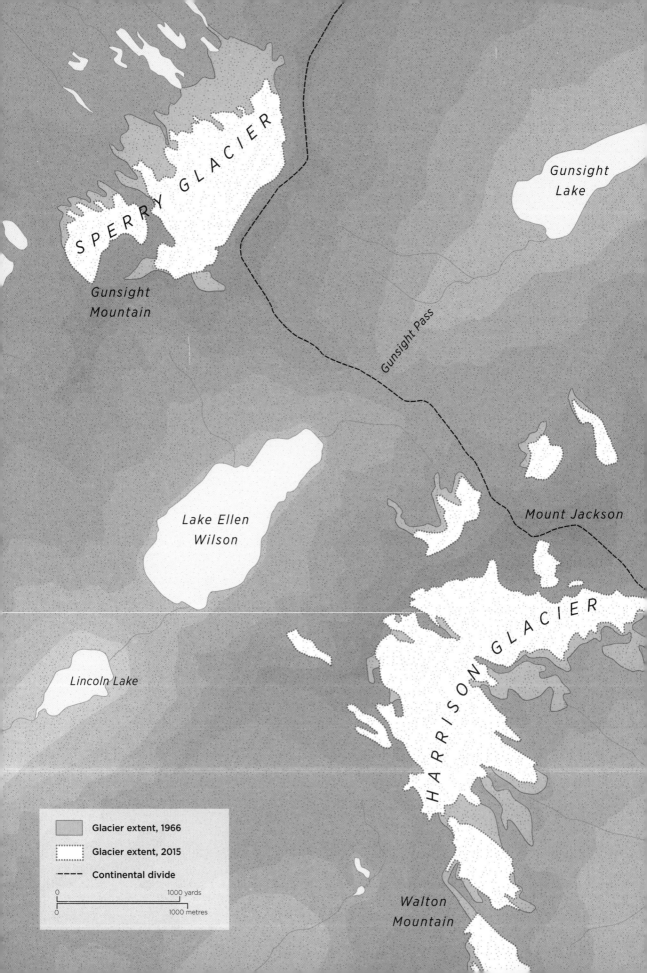

SPERRY GLACIER

Gunsight
Lake

Gunsight
Mountain

Gunsight Pass

Lake Ellen
Wilson

Mount Jackson

HARRISON GLACIER

Lincoln Lake

Walton
Mountain

Glacier extent, 1966

Glacier extent, 2015

Continental divide

0   1000 yards

0   1000 metres

St Mary River

0 ——— 10 miles
0 ——— 10 km

N

WATERTON LAKES
NATIONAL PARK

Thunderbird 21%

CANADA
USA

Agassiz 54%   Dixon 57%   Miche Wabun 49%
Kintla   Whitecrow 57%
33%   Weasel Collar   Old Sun 19%
        Rainbow   10%
        26%   Ahern 13%
                    Vulture
                     27%   GLACIER NATIONAL
                                                Grinnell 45%
                             PARK

St Mary River

Sperry   Jackson 41%
40%   Blackfoot 18%
                         Logan 56%
        map below
                         Pumpelly 10%
        Harrison 19%

Flathead River

MONTANA

Major glacier extent and
percentage loss (1966–2015)

ACKSON
GLACIER

BLACKFOOT GLACIER

PUMPELLY
GLACIER

Blackfoot
Mountain

N

A certain degree of ebb and flow is always to be expected with glaciers, but in the 1980s the US Geological Survey identified what they termed 'a continuous pattern of retreat' among the glaciers of Glacier National Park. More recent studies of the park's Harrison, Gem and Sperry Glaciers showed substantial increases in the rate of loss between 1966 and 2005, with the Sperry Glacier losing 35 per cent of its mass in that time and fresh lakes and moraines emerging where previously there was only solid ice. The causes are easy to identify but almost impossible to halt. Montana is warming at nearly twice the global average. Warmer winters mean that the Rockies today receive more rain than glacier-forming snow, and even when it does snow that snow and ice is melting faster with more clement spring weather arriving earlier and earlier. Unless the current conditions change, it is predicted that all of Glacier National Park's glaciers could be gone by 2030 and with them would go what was once championed as 'the best care-killing scenery on the continent'.

LEFT Warmer winters are threatening the survival of the Glacier National Park.

CHIHUAHUAN DESERT

MEXICO/USA

28° 58' 00.0" N / 105° 26' 06.0" W

With a name believed to derive from the Nahuatl for 'dry, sandy place' (and subsequently bestowed on a local breed of small, hairless pet dogs) you'd expect the Chihuahuan Desert to be quite deserted. This, after all, is North America's largest desert, and deserts, by and large, are typically arid places where a lack of living things (water, trees, people) tends to be fairly front and centre. But deserts, even the driest and least inviting to animals and plants, contain subtle multitudes. And rather like silences (outside of vacuums) and as John Cage demonstrated with his famous 4'33" piece, they are often noisy with life.

Sprawling across the American-Mexican border, from Arizona through southwestern Texas and far into Mexico, the Chihuahuan Desert runs close to 140,000 square miles (362,600 square kilometres). It is credited with being the third most biologically diverse desert in the world. And while possessing areas of parched earth that are particularly perilous to all concerned, the desert also contains stretches of stunning grasslands that provide habitat for birdlife, including soaring raptors and chestnut-collared longspurs, as well as sprinting pronghorn. There are rivers and streams that flit fitfully across the terrain and hot-spring wetlands that support species of fish such as the Julimes pupfish. On isolated mountain tops here and there, even ponderosa pine and maple trees can be spied, holding their heads up high, while the floor of the desert basin is a sea of creosote, yucca, cacti and succulents, of which there are over 300 different indigenous varieties.

The lifeblood of this ecosystem is the Rio Grande/Rio Bravo, the great river that flows between the two nations from Colorado to the Mexican Gulf and whose waters, along with some underground

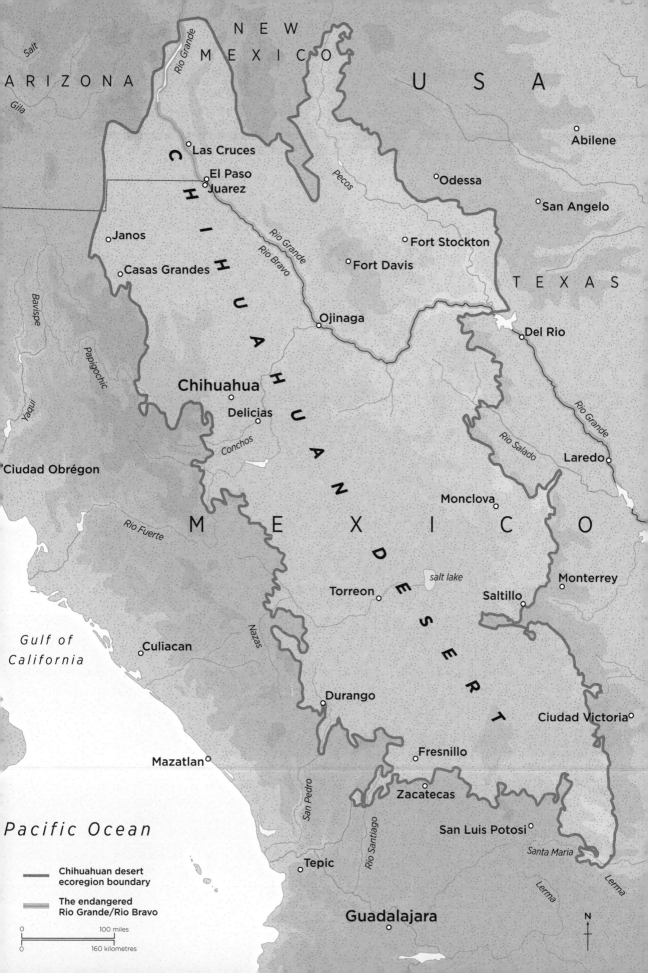

Salt

ARIZONA

Gila

NEW
MEXICO

USA

C

Abilene

Las Cruces

Odessa

El Paso
Juarez

San Angelo

H

Janos

Rio Grande

I

Pecos

Rio Bravo

Fort Stockton

Casas Grandes

Fort Davis

H

TEXAS

Bavispe

U

Ojinaga

Del Rio

Papigochic

A

Yaqui

Chihuahua

H

Rio Grande

Delicias

U

Rio Salado

Ciudad Obrégon

Conchos

A

Laredo

Rio Fuerte

MEXICO

N

Monclova

Monterrey

salt lake

Saltillo

Gulf of
California

Torreon

D

Culiacan

Nazas

E

Durango

S

Ciudad Victoria

E

Fresnillo

R

Mazatlan

San Pedro

Zacatecas

T

Pacific Ocean

Rio Santiago

San Luis Potosi

Santa Maria

Tepic

Lerma

Lerma

Chihuahuan desert
ecoregion boundary

The endangered
Rio Grande/Rio Bravo

Guadalajara

N

100 miles

160 kilometres

springs and the much-prayed-for summer rains, supply the only major sources of hydration here.

Yet the diversion of this precious resource towards agriculture and the irrigation of desert farms growing cash crops such as water-hungry alfalfa, pecan and cotton, and more generally to satisfying the demands of the region's growing population, has had serious consequences for the natural environment. Overgrazing and the conversion of grassland into plots for farms has resulted in soil erosion, the loss of habitats and food for wildlife. With temperatures peaking ever upwards and evaporating what precious little water there is that falls from the sky or is stored in the reservoirs, the Chihuahuan Desert is at risk of becoming decidedly more stereotypically desert-like unless more action is taken to prevent it.

RIGHT: In 2010, the bed of the Rio Grande/Rio Bravo in the Chihuahuan Desert near the village of San Antonio, New Mexico, was completely dry.

BELOW: The Rio Grande/Rio Bravo flowing through a canyon along the Mexican border in Texas, USA.

TIMBUKTU

MALI

16° 46′ 23.3″ N / 3° 00′ 31.2″ W

In its definition for 'Timbuktu' the Oxford English Dictionary offers that it is 'a town in north Mali' before adding that its name is often 'used in reference to a remote or extremely distant place'. 'You would hear the screams from here to Timbuktu' is just one of the examples it gives to help illustrate the point.

This association with being out of the way dates from the 1830s when European travellers finally reached this forbidding outpost on the southern edge of the Sahara. Along with earning a reputation for the remoteness of its locale, it soon entered the Victorian popular consciousness as somewhere exotic and romantically other-worldly. The poet Lord Alfred Tennyson saluted it in verse calling 'Timbuctoo' (in the spelling of the day) 'mysterious' and 'unfathomable' and comparing it to the lost world of Atlantis and the mythical city of gold, El Dorado.

But founded by Tuareg nomads in around 1100, Timbuktu, far from being obscure, was once at the centre of things. Created at the intersection of west African and trans-Saharan trade routes, it grew to be the richest settlement in the region, its wealth generated by brisk sales of salt, spices, gold and slaves. Although built on commerce, Timbuktu was also a seat of learning with several universities and many libraries, whose extremely rare manuscripts inscribed on parchment, tree bark or tanned antelope skin, survive in private collections locally, against the odds and the attentions of termites and dubious rare-book dealers.

By the fourteenth century it had become the true intellectual and spiritual capital for the propagation of Islam throughout Africa. Djingareyber, Timbuktu's main and oldest mosque, and the two smaller mosques, Sankore and Sidi Yahia, date back to this era,

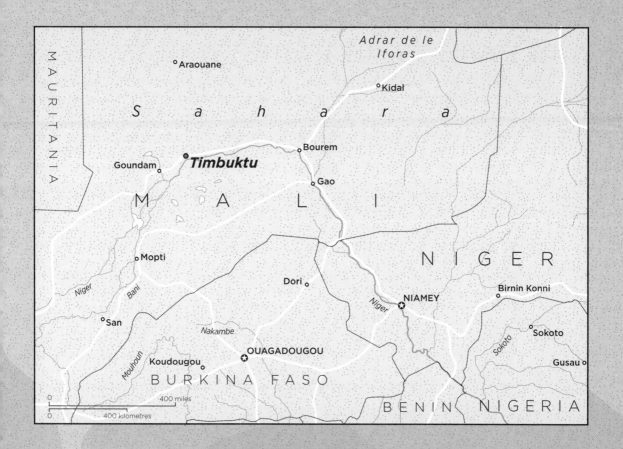

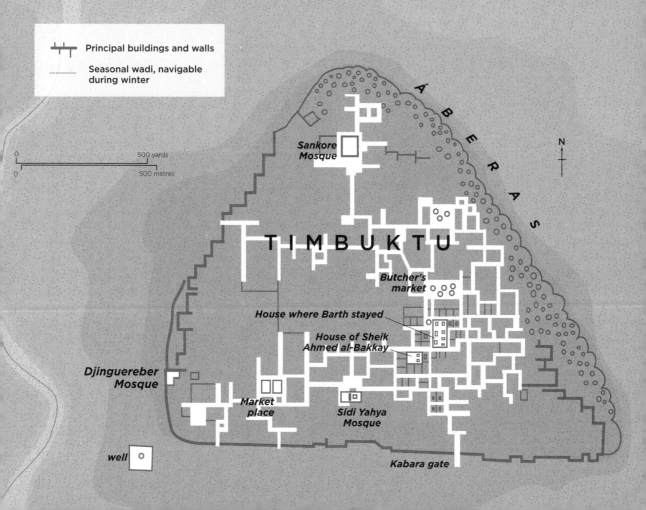

Principal buildings and walls

Seasonal wadi, navigable during winter

0 — 500 yards
0 — 500 metres

A B E R A S

N

Sankore Mosque

T I M B U K T U

Butcher's market

House where Barth stayed

House of Sheik Ahmed al-Bakkay

Djinguereber Mosque

Sidi Yahya Mosque

Market place

well ◦

Kabara gate

when they were also home to Islamic scholars known as the Ambassadors of Peace.

The mosques, like almost every other structure in Timbuktu until more recent concrete additions, were fashioned almost entirely from the local soil. The prime building material in these parts was banco – the local mud, sun baked with rice husks into building blocks and then finished off with more of the same, applied damp as a plaster; and the whole structure reinforced with timber. Djingareyber, which dominates the heart of the town, is accordingly a magnificent surreal sandcastle of a building with jagged turrets. Its minaret, spiky as a hedgehog with protruding poles, looks rather like a giant cartoon caveman's club into the bargain.

Grazed by the Saharan desert winds and diluted by the rain, these earthen mosques have, from the moment of their creation, needed to be constantly patched up and re-plastered to survive. These repairs have for centuries been undertaken annually, in a week-long ritual imbued with significant religious meaning and social value to the community. Nevertheless, such efforts have proved unable to keep pace with the advancing degradation. Djingareyber, whose palmwood-and-mud roof was in danger of collapsing, was added to UNESCO's list of buildings in peril in 1988.

BELOW: The restored Djingareyber Mosque.

Close to twenty years later, a charitable trust established by the Aga Khan, the spiritual head of the Ismaili Muslim diaspora, bankrolled a major restoration of Djingareyber. While attracting a few detractors, who feared for the integrity of the local architecture, their work has served to stem the decay for the time being.

Graver problems sadly have emerged since then. In 2012, Timbuktu was occupied by militant Islamic groups, led by al-Qaida and Ansar Dine, who regard Mali's ancient form of Islam as heretical. Fighters from Ansar Dine smashed up eight of its mausoleums and the door of the Sidi Yahia mosque. UN peacekeepers and the French military subsequently restored order but these buildings continue to be at risk from assaults by fundamentalists.

Climatic conditions also threaten their health. Half a century ago tributaries of the River Niger reached Timbuktu, now they lie some 6 miles (10km) away. The borassus palms that provided the beams for doors and the supporting timbers no longer grow here, hardwood from Ghana has to be imported to sustain these mesmerizing edifices in an area characterized by an ever-increasing aridity.

SKARA BRAE

ORKNEY

9° 02′ 55.4″ N / 3° 20′ 30.3″ W

Situated off the far northern tip of Scotland and on a latitude that is only 50 miles (80km) south of Greenland, the Orkney Islands are cursed with, what the Scottish antiquarian Hugh Marwick deemed, 'one of the vilest' climates 'under heaven'. As one online tourist guide to the islands notes, 'travel to and from Orkney remains, to this day, at the mercy of the weather'. Before the arrival of modern satellite technology, fog could – and frequently would – ground visiting air and sea craft for days. And a lingering and unsurmountable impediment to travel, and the most common disruptor of the islands' ferry services, continues to be the storm-force gales that sweep in from the Atlantic and across the North Sea on the more inclement months of the year. Months filled with days when the sun deigns to be visible for a brief few hours at best and leave the islands in near complete darkness, are not uncommon. Even on the mildest of summer days in June, when by contrast there is almost continual daylight, Orkney is rarely free from Force Three or Four scale gusts. Few visitors, having taken the two-hour ferry ride from Scrabster on the Scottish mainland, would not agree with Magnus Spence who in *The Climate of Orkney* (1908) concluded that, 'No other region in Great Britain can compare with it for the violence and frequency of its winds.' Since the Orkney Islands are largely treeless, too, there's not much by way of natural shelter to avoid the winds. Bracing is perhaps the politest word to use.

It was, indeed, a severe wind that is supposed to have first revealed the ruins of a prehistoric settlement on Mainland, the largest of Orkney's islands. For centuries, the village had lain completely buried under a sandy mound known as Skara Brae (or Skerrabra to the Orcadians) on the shore of the Bay of Skaill. But its long slumber

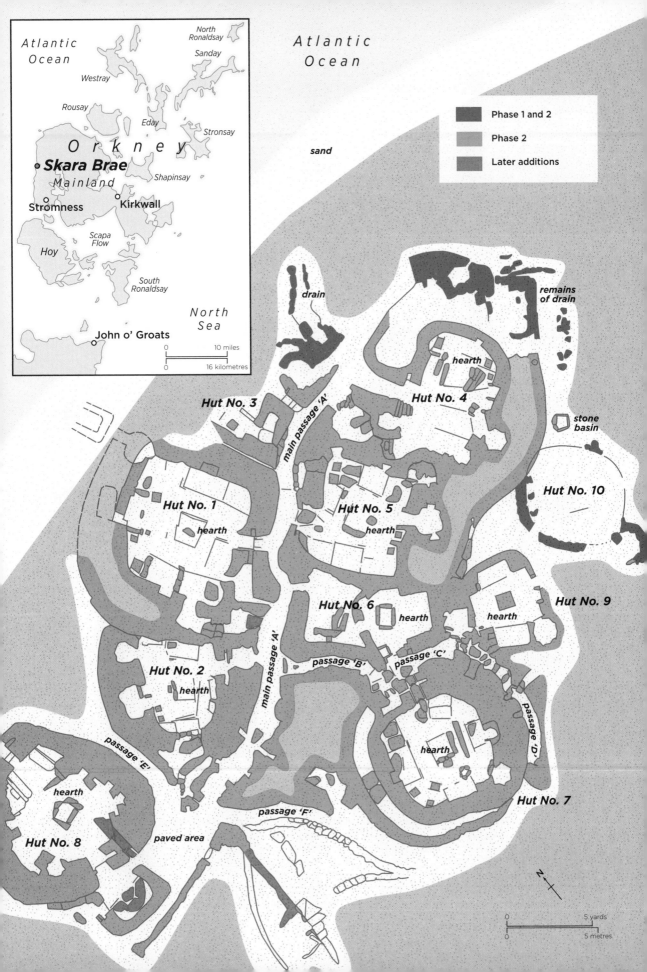

Atlantic Ocean

Atlantic Ocean

Phase 1 and 2

Phase 2

Later additions

sand

North Ronaldsay

Sanday

Westray

Rousay

Eday

Stronsay

O r k n e y

Skara Brae

Shapinsay

Mainland

Stromness

Kirkwall

Scapa Flow

Hoy

South Ronaldsay

North Sea

John o' Groats

0 — 10 miles

0 — 16 kilometres

drain

remains of drain

hearth

Hut No. 3

Hut No. 4

main passage 'A'

stone basin

Hut No. 10

Hut No. 1

hearth

Hut No. 5

hearth

Hut No. 6

hearth

hearth

Hut No. 9

main passage 'A'

passage 'B'

passage 'C'

Hut No. 2

hearth

passage 'D'

passage 'E'

hearth

passage 'F'

hearth

Hut No. 7

Hut No. 8

paved area

N

0 — 5 yards

0 — 5 metres

came to end one stormy night in February 1850. That evening, gale-force winds and the raging waves of the Atlantic swept along the western shoreline, causing the sand bank to collapse, ripping turf off the upper knoll and generally leaving gaping holes where there was once solid ground. In this instant, part of the island's Stone Age past abruptly broke into a Victorian steam-driven present, as sections of Neolithic dwellings were left poking out into the air. Or so the story goes. Contemporary meteorological reports seem to imply that there was nothing especially untoward about the weather for the dates in question. But then random heavy winds and crashing waves are what pass for normal on Orkney. Others argue that the ancient site was known long before 1850 and point to accounts of prehistoric discoveries on the island from at least 1769.

Still, whatever the truth of the storm story, the local landowner William Graham Watt, the 7th Laird of Skaill, initiated a series of excavations of the site in the 1860s. These included one led by James Farrer, dismissed in one history of Skara Brae as 'a notorious but sadly unmethodical antiquary', and another by the rather more meticulous George Petrie, an Orcadian antiquarian who was to present a detailed paper of his findings to the Society of Antiquaries of Scotland in 1867.

What they unearthed though, was a cluster of four circular dry-stone wall dwellings dating from between 3200 and 2000 BC and kitted out with astonishing, and remarkably well-preserved, interior furnishings – beds, chairs, shelves and a hearth – and a plethora of tools, pottery, beads and pendants, all fashioned, like the buildings themselves, entirely in stone.

After all the initial excitement generated by Skara Brae, whose 'dateless secrets' were even celebrated in verse, interest in the ruins seems to have waned after Petrie's time. No formal excavations would be carried out again until the 1920s. What spurred this renewed archaeological interest in Skara Brae was seemingly yet another bout of violent weather. Fearing that the ruins could be lost to the waves and the winds, a new sea wall was erected to protect the site in 1925 and the archaeologist Vere Gordon Childe was appointed to conduct fresh surveys, coming across a further four dwellings in the process, bringing the village's total to eight.

Childe was fascinated by what made the inhabitants of Skara Brae abandon it at some time around 2000 BC. Not only had these people seemingly walked away from their fine stone homes, they appeared also to have left a good portion of their most valued possessions behind as well. The presence of the latter, he suggested, was 'evidence of a hasty flight'. Others, in due course, would suggest that one feasible explanation for just such a flight could have been another earlier meteorological disaster. A storm, perhaps every bit as fierce as the one that later brought the village to light, laying waste to the island. While such a theory has symmetry on its side, it receives short shrift

PREVIOUS PAGE: Skara Brae's position on the coast makes it vulnerable to wind and sea.

BELOW: One of the circular stone dwellings.

from modern-day archaeologists. Far from making a rapid exit, it is now believed that the islanders probably left gradually, and over many years. This move was most likely sanctioned by the evolving nature of their tribal society and shifts in the landscape due to coastal erosion. Skara Brae itself originally stood some way inland before scouring tides claimed the ground before it.

The weather, nevertheless, poses an ever-present danger to Skara Brae. Rising sea levels and increasingly violent storms connected to climate change could now wipe it away just as swiftly as the winds that unearthed it all those years ago.

YAMUNA RIVER

INDIA

28° 39' 59.7" N / 77° 14' 16.3" E

The Yamuna, whose name derives from the Sanskrit 'yama' for a twin and nods to its parallel relationship with its better-known progenitor and the river into which it eventually merges, is the largest tributary of the Ganges. It flows for 850 miles (1,370km) from the Yamunotri glacier of Uttarkashi in Uttar Pradesh to Allahabad. Its waters, which Babur, the first Mughal emperor in the sixteenth century, described as 'better than nectar', have been venerated for thousands of years and provided prized royal elephants of ages past with the best means to clean up and cool off. The religiously inclined continue to bath in and drink from the river as an act of devotion. But far more prosaically, over sixty million Indians still rely on it as a principal, if not sole, source of hydration.

The Yamuna nourished the birth of the cities of Delhi, Mathura and Agra, which rose along its banks. And Shah Jahan, one of Babur's Mughal successors, chose to build one of India's most famous monuments, the Taj Mahal, on a sharp bend of the river at Agra. In 1978 the river broke its banks causing cataclysmic flooding that nearly put the entire city under water. But if floods continue to be a worry in certain places (the Taj Mahal was again seriously threatened in 2003 and in 2008), appalling pollution and near-yearly droughts, caused by the siphoning off of great swathes of the river for industrial and domestic uses, have long since supplanted them as the most pressing concern about the Yamuna.

Described, not unreasonably, as 'one of the dirtiest rivers on the planet', more than twenty drains dispense toxic chemicals and raw sewage directly into the Yamuna in Delhi, where the population has doubled since 1991. At Wazirabad, just inside the Delhi borders, one major drain reportedly pumps nearly 500 million gallons of sewage

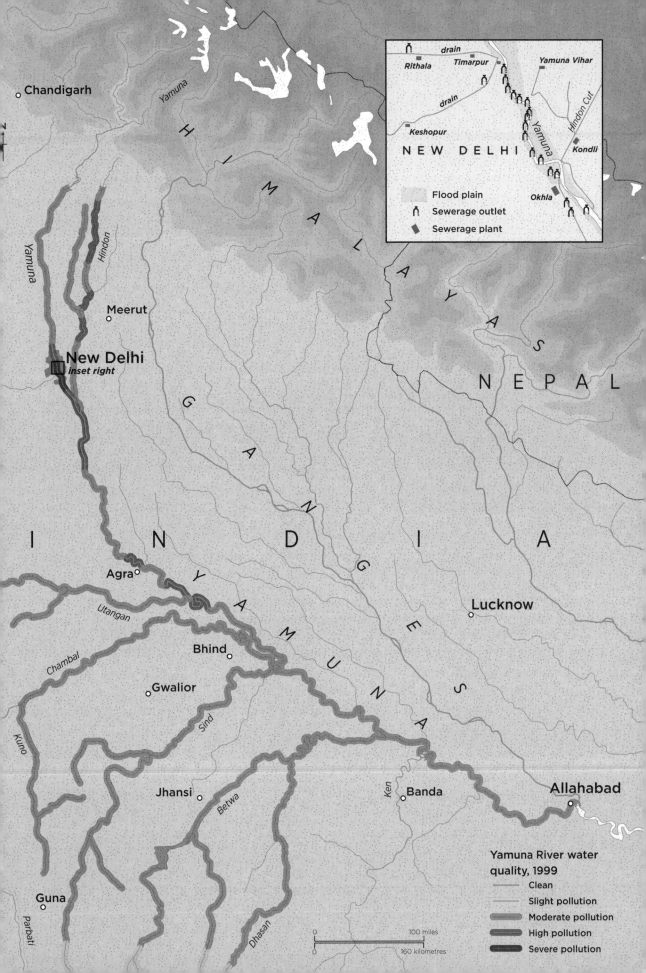

Chandigarh

Yamuna

HIMALAYAS

NEPAL

Meerut

Hindon

Yamuna

New Delhi
inset right

INDIA

Agra

Utangan

Chambal

NYAMUNA

GANGES

Lucknow

Bhind

Gwalior

Sind

Kuno

Jhansi

Betwa

Ken

Banda

Allahabad

Guna

Parbati

Dhasan

NEW DELHI (inset)

drain

Rithala   Timarpur   Yamuna Vihar

drain

Hindon Cut

Keshopur

NEW DELHI   Yamuna   Kondli

Okhla

Flood plain
Sewerage outlet
Sewerage plant

Yamuna River water quality, 1999

Clean
Slight pollution
Moderate pollution
High pollution
Severe pollution

0   100 miles

0   160 kilometres

into the river each day. Not far from there, the river is often choked by deposits of plastic, polythene, the waste leather cuttings from local shoe factories and assorted other rubbish. At Agra, the lack of fresh-flowing, clean water in the Yamuna is causing the Taj Mahal to yellow as the river is failing to absorb ambient air pollutants and other matter. For vast stretches of the river, oxygen levels drop to a deathly zero per cent. While Prime Minister Narendra Modi came to power in 2014 promising to revive the Yamuna, to date his government's efforts to rejuvenate the river have been easily surpassed by the rather more arbitrary monsoon rains of 2018. This downpour re-oxygenated its waters and flushed away other pollutants and, if only briefly, left the river 'at its healthiest in years'. The season having passed, however, pollutants were again on the rise and the river at present is just as environmentally imperilled as before.

ABOVE: Rubbish has accumulated on the banks of the Yamuna in New Delhi.

RIGHT: The Taj Mahal is starting to go yellow due to the poor state of the Yamuna river.

VENICE

ITALY

45° 26′ 02.3″ N / 12° 20′ 18.8″ E

Venice, or so the legend holds (and let's face it, few places on earth are quite as legendary as this island metropolis) was founded at midday on 25 March AD 421. This date fell on a Friday that year, as Jan Morris, one of the city's more trustworthy chroniclers, has ascertained by consulting the relevant calendars.

Venice is a place that inspires works of complete fiction, and a certain tendency for factual embellishment from even usually quite steadfast commentators, fittingly perhaps given its most famous building is the extravagantly byzantine basilica of St Mark's, which contains lavishly gilded mosaics that preach a story of religious salvation through humble devotion. Still, while the Old Testament God of Genesis might well have used the sixth day of the week to create all the creatures that lived on dry land, in the contemporary epoch Fridays, surely, are more readily associated with winding down than embarking on bold new exercises in urban development. Visit almost any office in the western world, and nearing lunchtime on a Friday is arguably when the productivity levels really start to dip. Friday afternoon meetings are invariably scheduled at their peril, or expressly to underscore the higher rank and authority of their mean-spirited schedulers. Still Giovanni Bono, or John the Good, the poor fisherman, and those with him on that particular Friday, who resolved to build a city in a malarial lagoon in the Adriatic Sea off the north-eastern coast of Italy, were evidently of firmer purpose. Their purpose, arguably, far firmer than the ground on which they had elected to erect this new municipality.

For leaving aside its creation myth, Venice is spread over 117 (or 118 by some accounts), different islands. This archipelago was formed

ABOVE: Surrounded by water, Venice has a long history of being susceptible to flooding, as seen in this 19th century illustration.

over 6,000 years ago when the streams of six rivers flowing down from the Alps, and carrying deposits of sand, shale and mud with them, reached this corner of the Adriatic Sea. The mingling of fresh river water and the salt of the sea created the lagoon, while the mountain sediment formed the islands on which this uniquely amphibious city would eventually arise. Protected from the ocean by a ridge of sand banks, its inhabitants for centuries were simple fisher folk and salt gatherers; their trades hovering, like the islands themselves, somewhere between water and land. These were people, too, for whom the rise of the Roman Empire on the mainland just a short distance away was largely a matter of indifference. Evidence of it was marked, even at its high pomp, mostly by the building of the odd villa as a retreat and the appearance of the occasional hunting party on offshore jollies after ducks. But it was Imperial Rome's misfortune, in particular the arrival of Germanic tribes, the Visigoths and Huns, who from the fourth century on swarmed across the empire sacking cities as they went, that was the making of Venice. It is as a place of refuge for those fleeing the mainland that the city's true origins lie. And throughout its history, this city, a republic from AD 697 until its eventual fall in the eighteenth century, would, in turn, offer sanctuary to successive waves of immigrants, embracing, in the words of one visitor, 'those who all

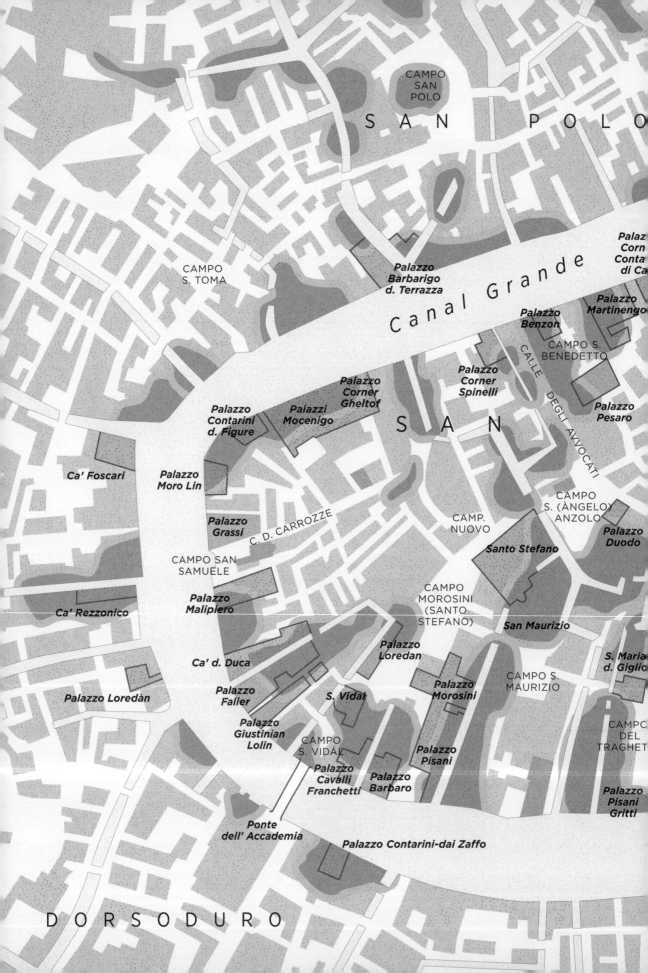

CAMPO
SAN
POLO

S A N   P O L O

CAMPO
S. TOMA

Palazzo
Barbarigo
d. Terrazza

Canal Grande

Palaz
Corn
Conta
di Ca

Palazzo
Benzon

Palazzo
Martinengo

CAMPO S.
BENEDETTO

Palazzo
Corner
Gheltof

Palazzo
Corner
Spinelli

S A N

Palazzo
Pesaro

CALLE   DEGLI   AVVOCATI

Palazzo
Contarini
d. Figure

Palazzi
Mocenigo

Ca' Foscari

Palazzo
Moro Lin

CAMPO
S. (ÀNGELO)
ANZOLO

Palazzo
Duodo

Palazzo
Grassi

C. D. CARROZZE

CAMP.
NUOVO

Santo Stefano

CAMPO SAN
SAMUELE

Ca' Rezzonico

Palazzo
Malipiero

CAMPO
MOROSINI
(SANTO
STEFANO)

San Maurizio

Ca' d. Duca

Palazzo Loredan

Palazzo
Falier

S. Vidal

Palazzo
Morosini

CAMPO S.
MAURIZIO

S. Maria
d. Giglio

Palazzo
Giustinian
Lolin

CAMPO
S. VIDÀL

Palazzo Pisani

CAMPO
DEL
TRAGHET

Palazzo
Cavalli
Franchetti

Palazzo
Barbaro

Palazzo
Pisani
Gritti

Ponte
dell' Accademia

Palazzo Contarini-dai Zaffo

D O R S O D U R O

Ponte
di Rialto

CAMPO S.
BARTOLOMEO

Fondaco
d. Tedeschi

SALIZZADA SAN LIO

MARZARIETA 2 APRILE

CASTELLO

Palazzo
Dolfin-
Manin

Palazzo
Giustinian
Faccanon

Palazzo
Bembo

S. Salvadore

CORTE
D. TEATRO

CALLE DEL CARBON

zzo
ani

CAMPO
S. LUCA

CALLE DEI FABBRI

MARZARIA
(MERCERIA)
S. ZULIAN

CALLE DEI FUSERI

CAMPO
MANIN

na
ini

M A R C O

Scala del
Bovolo

San Gallo

Torre dell'
Orologio

Palazzo
Patriarcale

San Marco

FREZZERIA

CAMPO
FANTÌN

atro
enice

Procuratie
Vecchie

Museo
Civico Correr

Campanile

PIAZZA
SAN MARCO

Palazzo
Ducale

Palazzo
Reale

PIAZZETTA
SAN
MARCO

C. LARGA XXII MARZO

CALLE VALLARESSO

Procuratie
Nuove

Biblioteca
Marciana

Columns of
San Marco &
San Todaro

Palazzo
Giustinian

Capit.
del
Porto

Palazzo Treves
Barozzi

Palazzo
Flangini
Fini

Venice Lagoon

Principal Venetian buildings with
substantial canal wall damage

Areas where flooding
occurs 10–50 times a year

Santa Maria della Salute

0   100 yards

0   100 metres

N

others shun' and affording 'welcome to those persecuted elsewhere'.

Gifted with plenty of salt, some sand and trees, but lacking both arable land and natural stone, Venice really had to be open to imports to flourish and grow in the first place. Geography, topography, temperament and financial necessity conspired to ensure its energies would always be turned outwards to maritime and international trade. Standing on the frontiers of the east and west, it would count Byzantine Constantinople and Islamic Cairo as trading partners and by the thirteenth century controlled 70 per cent of all the spices imported into Europe from Asia and beyond. The merchants of Venice were also able to call upon the assistance of the numerous banks and money-lenders who were free to operate within this city republic when such activities were heavily curtailed elsewhere in Europe.

This city of footpaths rather than streets, and canals rather than roads, abounds in the loss of its former glories, and so much of its beauty is ultimately and intimately entangled in the now faded excesses of earlier times. But currently those beauties are in danger from excesses of our own era. Tourism, although responsible for the saving of Venice as a going concern, has more recently threatened to ruin it. Crowds have grown so large over the holiday season that in 2018 the city authorities took the step of installing gates to control the flow of visitors to St Mark's Square and the Rialto Bridge. At the

BELOW: Large cruise ships such as this one bring huge numbers of tourists to Venice.

ABOVE: The rising waters in Saint Mark's Square during the seasonal Acqua Alta.

time of writing, the city is still considering further restrictions to the numbers of day trippers allowed in. A ban has also been proposed on mega yachts that have taken to mooring in the lagoon. Some of these vessels are so vast that their shadows put many of Venice's much-fabled sights into the shade. But in the autumn of 2018, three-quarters of Venice was flooded when the seasonal Acqua Alta (i.e. high water) tides rose to exceptional levels, leaving parts of the city knee-deep in water. Flooding is to Venice as rain and pigeons are to London and smog is to Los Angeles; an unpleasant but familiar enough nuisance. A mosaic in the western portico of Saint Mark's depicting the biblical flood and dating from the eleventh century suggests that Venetians have obviously long had encroaching waters on their minds. Yet the subsidence of the islands themselves by something like 10cm (4in) over the last century, rising sea levels and the increasingly frequency of floods due to now regular annual tidal swells, raises the very real prospect that within the next thirty years the waters could make Venice all but uninhabitable.

THE CONGO BASIN RAINFOREST

DEMOCRATIC REPUBLIC OF THE CONGO

0° 28′ 40.2″ S / 17° 45′ 49.6″ E

An immense tapestry of fetid swamps, muddy rivers, dense jungle, open woodland and grassy savannahs, the Congo Basin rainforest is twice the size of France and exceeded only in scale by the Amazon. Spanning six countries (while a further three have territory in its purlieu), by far the largest area of rainforest, some 60 per cent of it, is contained within the Democratic Republic of the Congo. A huge nation gifted with a vast stock of extremely valuable, natural mineral resources, the Republic is interrelatedly cursed with a troubled colonial past and no less traumatic contemporary history. Between 1997 and 2003, the country was engaged in a horrific civil war that left over six million people dead, with disease and malnutrition felling those not killed in the action itself. While the conflict raged, swathes of the forest were cleared by illegal loggers able to operate with impunity and, more often than not, even in collusion, overtly or covertly, with militias from factions on either side of the political divide. Though the war, for the most part and at the time of writing, is over, the harvesting of rainforest trees, such as the African mahogany, which is supposedly protected by both national and international law, shows no sign of abating. Forest clearances are only advancing and with worrying rapidity, if anything.

Research published in November 2018 by the University of Maryland's Department of Geographical Sciences revealed that the Congo Basin had lost around 64,000 square miles (165,000 square kilometres) of forest between 2000 and 2014. This amounts to the loss of an area larger than Bangladesh in less than fifteen years. By their estimation, if these rates of deforestation were to continue, the basin

ABOVE: Between 60 and 75 million people live in the Congo basin region, such as the ocupant of this hut in Kivu, the Democratic Republic of Congo

would be devoid of forest entirely by 2100. Others, however, have painted a gloomier picture still, noting that with a fivefold increase in the human population in the Congo Basin projected within the same period, it possibly might not even make it that long.

At present the forest, according to the World Wildlife Fund, boasts over 10,000 species of plants, more than 400 different types of mammal – among them bonobos, chimpanzees, mountain gorillas, forest elephants, okapi and buffalo – and at least a thousand birds, including Black-tailed godwits, whimbrels and Jack snipes. Ranks of the forest's great apes have already been devastated by outbreaks of the ebola virus in the last decade but long-term deforestation presents an appalling prospect for all its wildlife, much of which occurs nowhere else in the world.

Between 60 and 75 million people are believed to live in the Congo basin region, and that number has been calculated to grow by as much as 1.7 million a year, the majority of them, to a greater

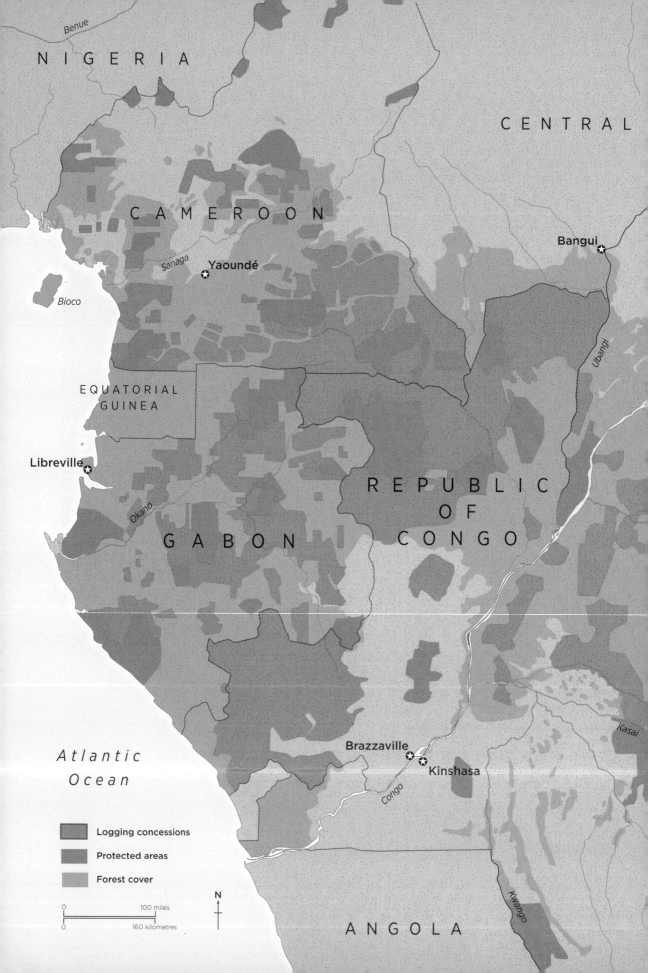

NIGERIA

Benue

CENTRAL

CAMEROON

Sanaga   **Yaoundé** ★

Bangui ★

Bioco

EQUATORIAL
GUINEA

Libreville ★

REPUBLIC
OF
CONGO

Okano

GABON

Ubangi

*Atlantic
Ocean*

Kasai

Brazzaville ★
★ **Kinshasa**

Congo

Logging concessions

Protected areas

Forest cover

Kwango

0 _____ 100 miles
0 _____ 160 kilometres

N

ANGOLA

and lesser extent, dependent on the forest for their food, shelter and livelihoods. And a perhaps surprisingly significant cause of damage to the rainforest's ecology has been the increase of small-scale subsistence cultivation. Here, innocently or not so innocently, modest tracts of the forest are cleared for agricultural plots of such staples as maize and cassava, which are farmed until all the nutrients of the soil are exhausted. Then another part of the forest is cleared and the process begins again, with a creeping trail of destruction inexorably growing bit by bit. Nevertheless, in comparison with these miniature operations, the revival of logging as a motor of the Republic's post-war economy, and the shift to industrial-scale production of crops such as palm oil requiring the wholesale removal of areas of forest, arguably pose a greater existential threat to its eventual survival. Since the forest is estimated to be the fourth largest carbon reservoir in the world and plays a vital role in regulating the globe's climate, its fate should concern us all, and deeply.

RIGHT: Felled tree trunks from the Congo Basin rainforest.

BELOW: Forest elephants are among the wildlife living in the Congo Basin rainforest that are under threat from deforestation.

THE GREAT BARRIER REEF

AUSTRALIA

18° 00′ 05.9″ S / 146° 50′ 03.4″ E

As the first Europeans to reach the eastern shores of Terra Australis Incognita, the 'Unknown Land of the South', Captain James Cook and the crew of HM Bark Endeavour were to become rather abruptly acquainted with the Great Barrier Reef.

Late on the evening of 10 June 1770, Cook himself having already turned in for the night, the Endeavour was sailing along the coast of far north Queensland. The sea was tranquil, the path ahead was illuminated by the glow of a full moon, and nothing on the horizon gave an indication of an imminent catastrophe when, bang, the ship hit a submerged coral outcrop. A fearful crunch of splintering timbers ensued, leaving in its wake a gaping hole in the underside of the ship and gallons of water from the Pacific Ocean rushing in. The crew rallied round and bailed the water out and finally managed to haul the stricken vessel ashore, where they would spend some seven weeks repairing it. They would, of course, meet the reef again many more times on this voyage, often encountering, as Cook recorded, a sheer 'wall of Coral Rock rising all most perpendicular out the unfathomable Ocean'. Here was a sublime thing, beautiful but horrifying, and potentially deadly to those in wooden boats attempting to navigate its more treacherous curlicues. Little wonder then that when Cook came to mark it on his ocean charts he labelled it the labyrinth, a word laden with rather sinister associations of imprisonment and getting hopelessly lost.

Cook was to give the western world its first descriptions of the reef. His impressions, published in his 1773 book, *An account of the voyages undertaken by order of his present Majesty for making discoveries in the southern hemisphere*, fuelled a public fascination with this extraordinary natural phenomenon that has never abated.

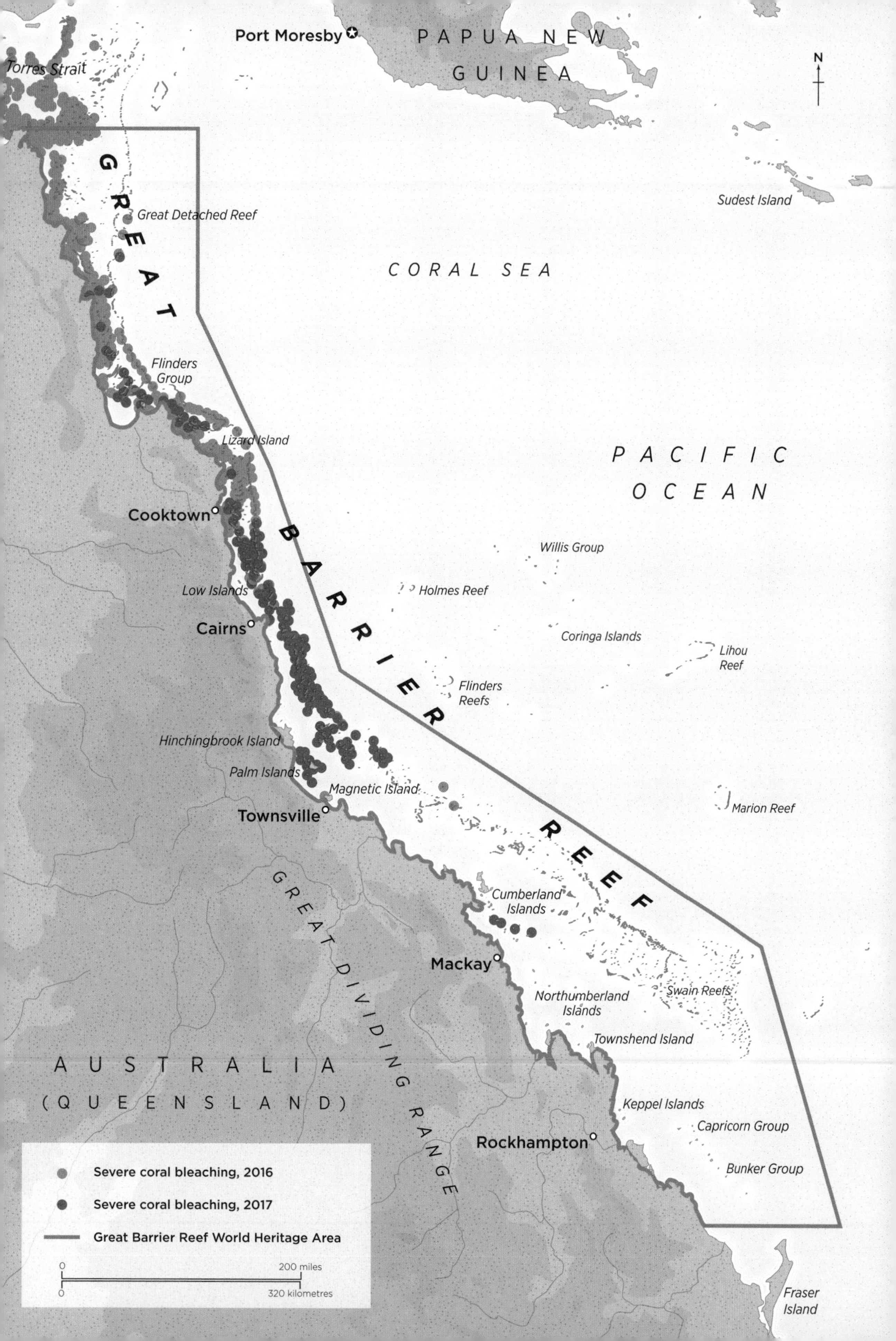

PAPUA NEW GUINEA

Port Moresby ✪

Torres Strait

G R E A T

Great Detached Reef

Flinders Group

Lizard Island

C O R A L   S E A

Sudest Island

Cooktown ○

B A R R I E R

Low Islands

Cairns ○

Willis Group

Holmes Reef

Coringa Islands

Lihou Reef

P A C I F I C
O C E A N

Hinchingbrook Island

Palm Islands

Magnetic Island

Flinders Reefs

Townsville ●

R E E F

Marion Reef

G R E A T   D I V I D I N G   R A N G E

Cumberland Islands

Mackay ●

Northumberland Islands

Townshend Island

Swain Reefs

A U S T R A L I A
(Q U E E N S L A N D)

Keppel Islands

Capricorn Group

Rockhampton ○

Bunker Group

Fraser Island

● Severe coral bleaching, 2016

● Severe coral bleaching, 2017

— Great Barrier Reef World Heritage Area

0 _____ 200 miles

0 _____ 320 kilometres

N

If anything, the more we learn about it, the more fascinating it becomes. Covering an area of 350,000 square miles (906,500 square kilometres), the Great Barrier Reef is larger than most of us realize, clocking in at about the same size as Japan and bigger than Great Britain and Ireland combined. Running for 1,243 miles (2,000km) along the northern coast of Australia, though not continuously but as a series of over 3,000 separate reefs, it is also the only living structure to be visible from space.

But far from living, parts of the coral, and especially those in the shallower habitats, have been dying at an alarming rate. In 2016, a nine-month-long marine heatwave, which raised the temperature of the Pacific Ocean to unprecedented high levels, destroyed the colourful algae on which coral feed, and resulted in the death of 30 per cent of the reef's coral from starvation and bleaching.

This distressing episode was repeated in the following year with a further 20 per cent of the reef's coral perishing in much the same circumstance. Historically the reef has always rebounded from similar bleaching, but with such high mortality rates, it appears doubtful that it will ever be able to recover what has been lost this time round. Coral reefs are immensely adaptable and some scientists maintain that this unique marine ecosystem will persist, but may only do so by adopting a different, perhaps diminished, form from the one it currently has. The greater concern is that unless something is done to reduce climate-induced rising sea temperatures – and the world's oceans are currently warming 40 per cent faster than previously thought – the reef will simply expire too rapidly for that to happen. Ultimately, it is us who have proven far more to deadly to the reef, than it is to us, as Captain Cook once assumed.

BELOW: An aerial view over the Great Barrier Reef, which is threatened by rising sea temperatures.

THE GREAT WALL

CHINA

40° 25′ 45.4″ N / 116° 33′ 59.2″ E

There is an ancient Chinese story that maintains that the first emperor of the Unified Kingdom of Qin obtained a magic carpet and rode to the moon to survey the extent of his dominions. Soaring high up into the heavens, the Emperor was at first filled with pride as he gazed down and saw all the lands that were his to command. But the more he looked, the more anxious he became. Just beyond his borders were peoples hostile to his own and the line between them appeared exceedingly thin when observed from above. Enemies seemed to threaten his empire from every direction. On returning to the earth he vowed to erect a gigantic barrier to keep the barbarians out and his own subjects in. And this, or so the ancient story goes, is the how the Great Wall of China, a structure itself famously possible to see from space, came to be built.

But as the photographer Daniel Schwartz has rightly observed, there is no Great Wall of China per se. The name in English refers to a system of different walls that were put up constantly over a period of more than 2,000 years. Great, though, it certainly is. As the longest manmade construction ever undertaken and stretching around one-twentieth of the circumference of the Earth, the Great Wall remains a totem of Chinese civilization.

As a feat of engineering, the scale and ambition of its execution continue to amaze. For the wall was neither a simple defensive bulwark nor a mere territorial marker, though in places it was both, but also a line of communication with over 10,000 beacons, at least 1,000 fortresses and many fortified gates and garrisons; the whole thing rising and falling along mountain peaks, weaving across grassy plains and spanning the Gobi Desert. Its architectural style varied in response to local topographical conditions and the materials to hand to produce

ABOVE: A decayed part of
the Great Wall between
Jinshangling and Simatai.

a wall in harmony with the surroundings. In the Gobi Desert, for instance, the wall is made up of layers of red palm fronds, reeds and gravel and much of it elsewhere is composed of natural earthworks.

The earliest parts of the wall date back to at least the seventh century BC. But it was upon the arrival of the first Qin Emperor, who took power in 217 BC and successfully unified the country, that its true construction is usually dated. The first Qin Emperor didn't need a magic carpet ride to know of the dangers posed to his still fragile empire by the non-Chinese Xiongnu (usually taken to be Germanic Huns) who lay to the north of his country, and equally the simmering regional power disputes that continued within it. The wall he advanced was therefore to bind together the disparate peoples under his rule by removing and supplanting earlier tribal border lines and excluding hostile alien intruders. It would stretch for some 10,000 li, or Chinese miles (roughly a third of an English mile). To this day the whole wall is known in its native land as The Ten Thousand Li Wall in honour of the Emperor's original and extraordinary structure.

That structure would be embellished upon and augmented by further walls over the subsequent ten dynasties, with the Han, Jin and Ming empires adding most to its scale. Under the Han dynasty the wall nearly doubled in size reaching the west bank of the Yellow River and the interior of Xingiang province. The last and most protracted work on the wall was undertaken in the Ming period when building techniques had advanced considerably, with the result that the bulk of what we think of as the Great Wall is mostly composed of brick-

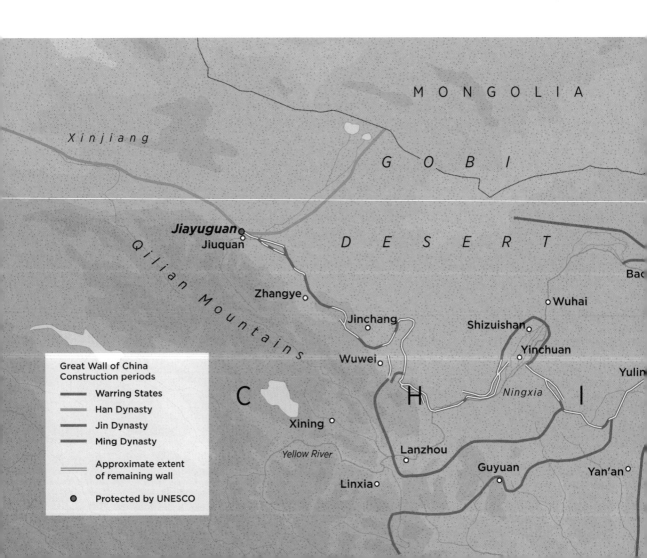

finished sections completed at that time. It is to a restored section of Ming wall at Badaling to the north of Beijing that most western tourists are escorted to admire the brilliance of the Chinese construction.

Yet even parts of this Ming wall are presently in danger of joining the largely lost eastern section of the wall that once headed towards the Korean Peninsula. Some 30 per cent, or 1,243 miles (2,000km), of the fortifications built in the Ming period are estimated to have disappeared already. Natural erosion and human damage, with decorative stones, in particular, pilfered and sold as souvenirs, are cited as the major and growing causes of destruction. A survey of the structure as a whole completed in 2014, found that 74.1 per cent of it was 'poorly preserved', while in 2018 a section of the wall in Ningxia was bulldozed for farmland by a local government department and seemingly with no serious censure from the national authorities. While the ruling Communist Party had formerly exhorted the Chinese people to 'Love the Motherland and Rebuild the Great Wall', at the time of writing experts express worry that far too little is being done to prevent much of what still stands from crumbling to dust.

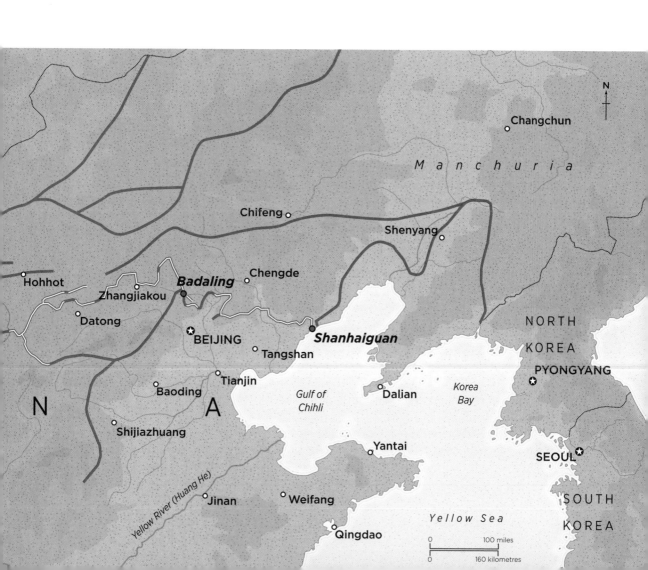

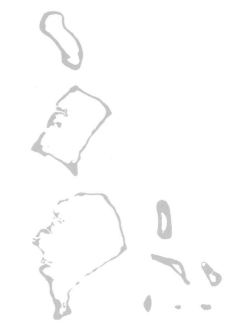

TUVALU

SOUTH PACIFIC

8° 31' 15" S / 179° 11' 55" E

A recent documentary on the plight of Tuvalu – by some accounts the fourth smallest nation on earth and comprised of six coral atolls and three reef islands flung across several thousand square miles of the South Pacific between Hawaii and Australia – was titled, and with droll wit, *That Sinking Feeling*. Standing no higher than 4.5m (15ft) above sea level, for thirty years the islands of Tuvalu have borne the United Nations' 1989 judgement that they are one of the 'most likely groups to disappear beneath the ocean in the 21st century because of global warming'.

In the decades since then an increasingly warmer and rising Pacific Ocean has nibbled away at the coral reefs that act as a protective fringe to the islands; epic King Tides have become more common and persistent visitors to their shores, also nosing, more often than not, into people's homes. The ever-more intrusive briny seawater meanwhile has also ruined the pulaka gardens and taro-growing pits – both plants once almost sole staples of traditional Tuvalu cuisine.

Following such a grim prognosis of their future prospects and these more tangible signs of the islands dissolving before their eyes, around a fifth of Tuvalu's 12,000 residents have opted to leave, the majority heading to New Zealand where the Tuvaluan community has tripled since 1996.

Possessing a total land mass of a mere 16 square miles (40 square kilometres), Tuvalu, which gained independence from the UK in 1978, has been inhabited for over 2,000 years. It also has almost all the elements of a picture postcard of a Pacific island paradise. The climate (King Tides and storms aside) is warm and tropical. The pellucid waters are blue and teeming with exotic fish and sea turtles. The beaches are sandy and dotted with coconut trees. And life (on the

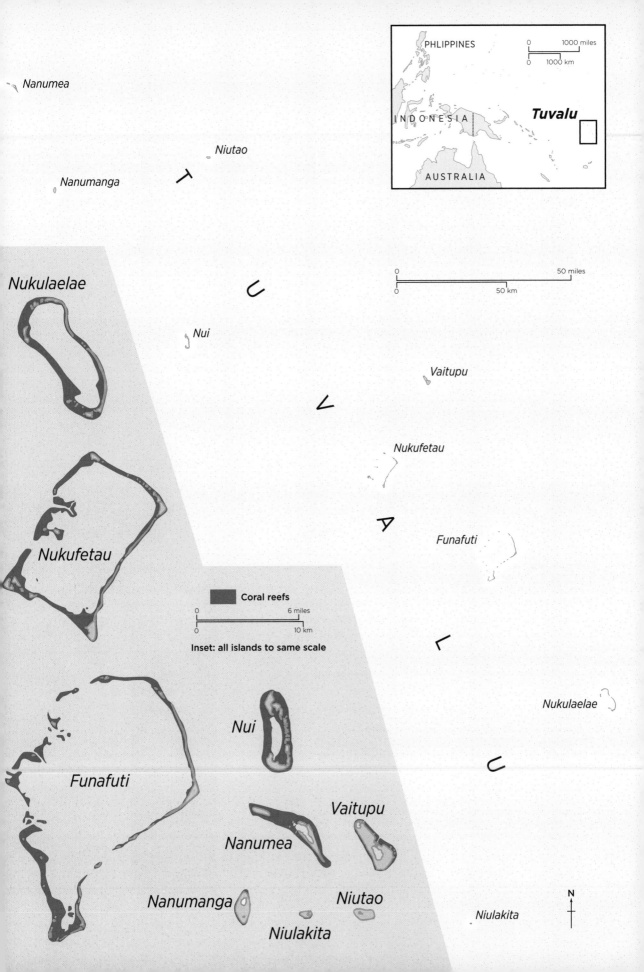

Nanumea

PHLIPPINES

INDONESIA

AUSTRALIA

Tuvalu

0   1000 miles
0   1000 km

Niutao

Nanumanga

Nukulaelae

Nui

Vaitupu

0   50 miles
0   50 km

Nukufetau

Nukufetau

Funafuti

■ Coral reefs

0   6 miles
0   10 km

Inset: all islands to same scale

Nukulaelae

Nui

Funafuti

Vaitupu

Nanumea

Nanumanga

Niutao

Niulakita

Niulakita

N

surface at least) appears easy, unhurried, positively languid if anything, with swimming, fishing, basket-weaving, woodcarving and folk dancing among the most frenetic activities observable there.

If rich in natural beauty, the islands are nevertheless relatively poor when it comes to saleable resources, with copra (dried coconut kernels) the only main export – and one also seriously at risk from soil salinization. Tuvalu's chief source of income hails from licensing its highly desirable internet domain, .tv, to an American company. During the Second World War, Tuvalu had actually served as a base for US forces who launched an assault on Japanese-held Tarawa from the Ellice Islands, as they were known then. Ecologists have also blamed wartime quarrying of the coral reef to build a runaway and ill-sighted defensive sea walls, the latter long since washed away, for contributing to much of the subsequent erosion of the lagoon-front at Funafuti, the largest island.

Those seeking less-worn tourist paths could hardly find anywhere better. In 2016 a report by the United Nations World Tourism Organization (UNWTO) found Tuvalu 'the least visited place on the planet', after it clocked up a mere 2,000 visitors that year. But with even its most loyal citizens facing up to the very real possibility of the wholesale abandonment of their islands, the time left to see them at all is fast vanishing.

Though reports of Tuvalu's demise others have argued are premature. A study by the University of Auckland and published in the journal *Nature Communications* in 2018, maintained that the atolls far from shrinking have, overall gained ground, with rising waves actually depositing more sediment onto their shores. Though the study's authors accepted that if the islands' future fate was possibly less doom-y than previously predicted, the march towards depopulation was already well advanced.

RIGHT: An American tank left on Funafuti after the Second World War.

BELOW: Funafuti Atoll is one of the most at-risk islands of Tuvalu, at just 4.5m (15ft) above sea level at its highest point.

SELECTED BIBLIOGRAPHY

This publication owes an enormous debt to numerous other books and articles. This select bibliography will, hopefully, give credit where credit is due and point those who want to know more in the right direction.

Ackroyd, Peter. *Venice: Pure City,* Chatto & Windus, London, 2009

Ahmed, Nazimuddin. *The Buildings of Khan Jahan in and around Bagerhat,* University Press, Dhaka, 1989

Anderson, Darren. *Imaginary Cities: A Tour of Dream Cities, Nightmare Cities, and Everywhere in Between,* Influx Press, London, 2015

Anthony, David W. (ed.). *The Lost World of Old Europe: The Danube Valley 5000-3500BC,* Princeton University Press, Princeton and Oxford, 2010

Ashton, John. *The Fleet: Its River, Prison, and Marriages,* T. Fisher Unwin, London, 1888 [1887]

Bahn, Paul G. (ed.). *Lost Cities,* Weidenfeld & Nicolson, London, 1997

Bandinelli, Ranuccio Bianchi. *The Buried City: Excavations at Leptis Magna,* Weidenfeld & Nicolson, London, 1966

Beattie, Andrew. *The Danube: A Cultural History,* Signal Books, Oxford, 2010

Bedell-Harper, Kempton. *Lost to the Sea: The Vanishing Coastline of Holderness,* Heritage Centre, Hull, September 1983

Beresford, M. W. *The Lost Villages of Yorkshire,* The Yorkshire Archæological Journal, 1952

Bergreen, Laurence. *Marco Polo: From Venice to Xanadu,* Quercus, London, 2007

Bolton, Tom (photography by Said, S.F.). *London's Lost Rivers: A Walker's Guide,* Strange Attractor, Devizes, 2014

Bright, Michael. *1001 Natural Wonders You Must See Before You Die,* Cassell Illustrated, London, 2005

Bristol, George. *Glacier National Park: A Culmination of Giants,* University of Nevada Press, Reno (Nevada), 2017

Browning, Iain. *Petra (Revised Edition),* Chatto & Windus, London, 1989

Caffarelli, Erneto Vergara and Caputo, Giacomo (translated from the Italian by Ridgway, David). *The Buried City: Excavations at Leptis Magna,* Weidenfeld & Nicholson, London, 1966

Carr, Archie. *The Everglades,* Time-Life Books, New York, 1973

Carr, Robert S. and Harrington, Timothy A. *The Everglades,* Arcadia Publishing, Charleston (North Carolina), 2012

Chaudhury, N.C. *Mohenjo-daro and the Civilization of Ancient India with References to Agriculture*, Bharatiya Publishing House, Varanasi, 1979

Childe, Vere Gordon. *Ancient Dwellings at Skara Brae,* Edinburgh, 1950

Childe, Vere Gordon. *Skara Brae*, H.M.S.O., Edinburgh, 1983

Clarke, David. *Skara Brae,* Historic Scotland, Edinburgh, 2012

Coombes, J.W. *The Seven Pagodas,* Seeley, Service and Company, London, 1914

Cornell, Tim and Mathews, John. *Atlas of the Roman World,* Phaidon, Oxford, 1982

Darnhofer-Demár, Edith. 'Colombia's Lost City Revealed' in *New Scientist,* Vol. 94, 20 May 1982

Dodson, Carolyn (illustrations by DeWitt Ivey, Robert). *A Guide to Plants of the Northern Chihuahuan Desert,* University of New Mexico Press, Albuquerque, 2012

El-Abbadi, Mostafa. *The Life and Fate of the Ancient Library of Alexandria,* UNESCO, Paris, 1990

English, Charlie. *The Book Smugglers of Timbuktu: The Race to Reach the Fabled City and the Fantastic Effort to Save its Past,* William Collins, London, 2017

Fetherling, Douglas. *The Gold Crusades: A Social History of Gold Rushes, 1849–1929,* Macmillan of Canada, Toronto, 1988

Finley, M. I. *Atlas of Classical Archeology,* Chatto & Windus, London, 1977

Fryer, Jonathan. *The Great Wall of China,* New English Library, London, 1975

Fullam, Brandon. *The Lost Colony of Roanoke: New Perspectives,* McFarland & Company, Jefferson (North Carolina), 2017

Geil, William Edgar. *The Great Wall of China,* John Murray, London, 1909

Grimal, Pierre (translated by Woloch, Michael). *Roman Cities,* University of Wisconsin Press, London and Wisconsin, 1983

Grunwald, Michael. *The Swamp: The Everglades, Florida, and the Politics of Paradise,* Simon & Schuster, New York, 2007

Haberman, David L. *River of Love in an Age of Pollution: The Yamuna River of Northern India,* University of California Press, Berkeley and London, 2006

Hanks, Donoh (ed.). *North-Carolina-Roanoke Island 1937, Official Illustrated Booklet: 350th Anniversary of Sir Walter Raleigh's Colony on Roanoke Island the Birth of the Virginia Dare,* Manteo (North Carolina), 1937

Haywood, John et al. *The Cassell Atlas of World History: The Ancient and Classical Worlds Volume One,* Cassell, London, 2000

Hirst, Anthony and Silk, Michael (eds.). *Alexandria, Real and Imagined,* Routledge, London, 2017

Hoare, Alison L. *Clouds on the Horizon: The Congo Basin's Forests and Climate Change,* Rainforest Foundation, London, 2007

Horn, James. *A Kingdom Strange: The Brief and Tragic History of the Lost Colony of Roanoke,* Basic Books, New York, 2010

Howe, Ellic. *A Short Guide to the Fleet River,* T. C. Thompson & Son, London, 1955

Hunwick, John O. *The Hidden Treasures of Timbuktu: Historic City of Islamic Africa,* Thames & Hudson, London, 2008

Jenkins, Mark. *To Timbuktu,* Robert Hale, London, 1998

Kench, Paul S. et al. 'Patterns of Island Change and Persistence Offer Alternate Adaptation Pathways for Atoll Nations' in *Nature Communications,* Article 605, February 2018

Kreiger, Barbara. *The Dead Sea: Myth, History, and Politics,* Brandeis University Press, Hanover (New Hampshire) and London, 1997

MacLeod, Roy (ed.). *The Library of Alexandria: Centre of Learning in the Ancient World,* I. B. Tauris, London, 2000

Magris, Claudio. *Danube,* Harvill Press, London, 2001

Mallet, Victor. *River of Life, River of Death: The Ganges and India's Future,* Oxford University Press, Oxford, 2017

Marken, Damien B. (ed.). *Palenque: Recent Investigations at the Classic Maya Center,* Altamira Press, Lanham (Maryland) and Plymouth, 2007

Markoe, Glenn (ed.). *Petra Rediscovered: Lost City of the Nabataeans,* Thames & Hudson, London, 2003

Matthews, David Kenneth. *Cities in the Sand. Leptis Magna and Subratha in Roman Africa,* University of Pennsylvania Press, Philadelphia, 1957

Mayes, Philip. *Port Royal Jamaica: Excavations 1969-70,* Jamaica National Trust Commission, Kingston (Jamaica), 1972

Michaud, Roland (photography by Michaud, Roland & Sabrina; text by Jan, Michel). *The Great Wall of China,* Abbeville Press Publishers, New York, 2001

Minetor, Randi. *Historic Glacier National Park: The Stories Behind One of America's Great Treasures,* LP, Guilford (Connecticut), 2016

Morris, Jan. *Venice,* Faber, London, 1974 [2015 edition]

Moseley, Michael E. and Day, Kent C. (eds.). *Chan Chan, Andean Desert City,* University of New Mexico Press, Albuquerque, 1982

Mountfort, Guy. *Portrait of a River: The Wildlife of the Danube, from the Black Sea to Budapest,* Hutchinson, London, 1962

Muir, Richard. *The Lost Villages of Britain,* History, Stroud, 2009

Niemi, Tina M. (ed.). *The Dead Sea: The Lake and its Setting,* Oxford University Press, New York and Oxford, 1997

Norwich, John Julius (ed.). *Cities that Shaped the Ancient World,* Thames & Hudson, London, 2014

Paine, Lauren. *Benedict Arnold, Hero and Traitor,* Robert Hale, London, 1965

Powell, Andrew Thomas. *Grenville and the Lost Colony of Roanoke: The First English Colony of America,* Matador, Leicester, 2011

Rababeh, Shaher M. *How Petra was Built: An Analysis of the Construction Techniques of the Nabataean Freestanding Buildings and Rock-Cut Monuments in Petra, Jordan,* Archaeopress, Oxford, 2005

Read, Peter. *Returning to Nothing: The Meaning of Lost Places,* Cambridge University Press, Cambridge, 1996

Rotherham, Ian D. *Yorkshire's Viking coast,* Amberley, Stroud, 2015

Sanday, John et al. *Bangladesh: Master Plan for the Conservation and Presentation of the Ruins of the Buddhist Vihara at Paharpur and the Historic Mosque-City of Bagerhat,* Unesco, Paris, 1983

Schwartz, Daniel. *The Great Wall of China,* Thames & Hudson, London and New York, 1990

Sheppard, Charles. *The Biology of Coral Reefs,* Oxford University Press, Oxford, 2018

Silverman, Helaine and Isbell, William (eds.). *Handbook of South American Archaeology,* Springer, New York, 2008

Sprague, Marguerite. *Bodie's Gold: Tall Tales and True History from a California Mining Town,* University of Nevada Press, Reno (Nevada) and Eurospan, London, 2003

Stambaugh, John E. *The Ancient Roman City,* Johns Hopkins University Press, Baltimore, 1988

Stuart, David and Stuart, George. *Palenque Eternal City of the Maya,* Thames & Hudson, London, 2008

Taylor, Jane. *Petra and the Lost Kingdom of the Nabataeans,* I.B. Tauris, London, 2001

Testi, Arnaldo (translated by Mazhar, Noor Giovanni). *Capture the Flag: The Stars and Stripes in American History,* New York University Press, New York, 2010

Thomsen, Clint. *Ghost Towns: Lost Cities of the Old West,* Shire Publications, Botley, Oxford, 2012

Urban, G. and Jansen, M. (eds.). *The Architecture of Mohenjo-Daro,* Books & Books, New Delhi, 1984

Wade, Stephen. *Lost to the Sea: Britain's Vanished Coastal Communities: Norfolk and Suffolk,* Pen & Sword History, Barnsley, South Yorkshire, 2017

Wade, Stephen. *Lost to the Sea: Britain's Vanished Coastal Communities: The Yorkshire Coast & Holderness,* Pen & Sword History, Barnsley, South Yorkshire, 2017

Weeden, Mark and Ullmann, Lee Z. (eds.), maps by Homan, Zenobia. *Hittite Landscape and Geography,* Brill Publishers, Leiden and Boston, 2017

PICTURE CREDITS

14–15 SM Rafiq Photography/Getty Image; 15 t SM Rafiq Photography/Getty Image; 18 t Gazi Nogay/Anadolu Agency/Getty Image; 18 b Marka/UIG via Getty Images; 22 Sklifas Steven/ Alamy Stock Photo; 24–25 Look/Alamy Stock Photo; 29 Granger Historical Picture Archive/ Alamy Stock Photo; 30 Yavuz Sariyildiz/Alamy Stock Photo; 31 beibaoke/Shutterstock. com; 34–35 Joerg Steber/ Shutterstock.com; 37 Joerg Steber/Shutterstock.com; 40 Dinodia Photos/Alamy Stock Photo; 41 Dittz/Shutterstock.com; 43 t Richard Maschmeyer/Alamy Stock Photo; 43 b Emiliano Rodriguez/Alamy Stock Photo; 45 t Roger Viollet/Getty Images; 46–47 Diego Grandi/Alamy Stock Photo; 50 Bibliotheque des Arts Decoratifs, Paris, France/ Archives Charmet/Bridgeman Images; 49 Original information courtesy The Helike Project; 51 © The Helike Project, Dora Katsonopoulou Director; 53 Shawshots/Alamy Stock Photo; 56 Boris Stroujko/Shutterstock.com; 57 Stuart Black/Alamy Stock Photo; 59 Robert Preston Photography/Alamy Stock Photo; 62–63 Mary Evans/Grenville Collins Postcard Collection; 63 t Anton_Ivanov/Shutterstock.com; 66 Hulton Archive/Getty Images; 68 t Sueddeutsche Zeitung Photo/Alamy Stock Photo; 68–69 Yasser El Dershaby/Shutterstock.com; 75 t Walkabout Photo Guides/Shutterstock.com; 75 b Porky Pies Photography/Alamy Stock Photo; 79 t Science History Images/Alamy Stock Photo; 80 Sarah Stierch (CC BY 4.0); 81 William S. Kuta/Alamy Stock Photo; 84 t dave stamboulis/Alamy Stock Photo; 84 b NazrulIslam/Shutterstock.com; 88 Chronicle/Alamy Stock Photo; 91 SnvvSnvvSnvv/Shutterstock.com; 96 The Sydney Morning Herald/Fairfax Media via Getty Images; 102 Niday Picture Library/Alamy Stock Photo; 103 Archive Farms Inc/Alamy Stock Photo; 107 World History Archive/Alamy Stock Photo; 109 Original information courtesy The Lost Sea; 110–11 © The Lost Sea; 115 shutterupeire/ Shutterstock.com; 118 Petersent (public domain); 120–21 Dead River Area Historical Society; 126 DEA/ICAS94/Getty Images; 128 travelview/Shutterstock.com; 129 Pavel Pavalanski/Alamy Stock Photo; 132 Dan Yeger/Alamy Stock Photo; 134–36 Sean Pavone/Alamy Stock Photo; 138 John Zada/Alamy Stock Photo; 139 Minden Pictures/Alamy Stock Photo; 140–41 Matthew J Thomas/Shutterstock.com; 145 Mary Evans Picture Library; 149 Tom Stack/Alamy Stock Photo; 153 Trougnouf (Benoit Brummer) (CC BY-SA 4.0); 156 Joe Mabel (CC BY-SA 2.0); 160–61 reisegraf.ch/Shutterstock.com; 161 Witold Skrypczak/Alamy Stock Photo; 164 DemarK/Shutterstock.com; 165 Chronicle/Alamy Stock Photo; 168–69 Ian Dagnall/ Alamy Stock Photo; 171 Jule_Berlin/Shutterstock.com; 174 clicksabhi/Shutterstock.com; 175 Alexander Helin/Alamy Stock Photo; 177 Mary Evans Picture Library; 180 Rolf_52/ Shutterstock.com; 181 irisphoto1/Shutterstock.com; 183 Universal Images Group North America LLC/DeAgostini/Alamy Stock Photo; 186–87 Education Images/UIG via Getty Images; 187 Edward Parker/Alamy Stock Photo; 190–91 Larissa Dening/Shutterstock.com; 193 P. Seydel/Shutterstock.com; 199 t Ashley Cooper/Alamy Stock Photo; 199 b Ashley Cooper/Corbis via Getty Images.

ACKNOWLEDGEMENTS

Thanks, first, to Lucy Warburton who commissioned this book, along with my previous two atlases, before departing for pastures new this time round. Thanks then to Julia Shone, who picked up the baton from Lucy and ensured we got the thing over the finishing line. Also invaluable in moving the book from manuscript to published entity were the managing editor Laura Bulbeck and Alison Moss, who as copyeditor wielded the red pen with aplomb. This book could hardly dare to be called an atlas without its maps, which were once again drawn with skill by my cartographical collaborator Martin Brown.

Further thanks to everyone at the pride of White Lion, for their efforts on behalf of this book and especially Melody Odusanya for publicity.

Thanks to the staff and librarians at The British Library in St Pancras and The London Library in St James's and Hackney Libraries, Stoke Newington branch.

And in addition I'd like to thank, friends, ancient and modern, my folks and family on either side of the Atlantic and my brilliant and beautiful wife, Emily Bick and our cat Phoebe.

INDEX

Brimming with creative inspiration, how-to projects and useful information to enrich your everyday life, Quarto Knows is a favourite destination for those pursuing their interests and passions. Visit our site and dig deeper with our books into your area of interest: Quarto Creates, Quarto Cooks, Quarto Homes, Quarto Lives, Quarto Drives, Quarto Explores, Quarto Gifts, or Quarto Kids.

First published in 2019 by White Lion Publishing,
an imprint of The Quarto Group.
The Old Brewery, 6 Blundell Street
London, N7 9BH,
United Kingdom
T (0)20 7700 6700
www.QuartoKnows.com

A catalogue record for this book is available from the British Library.

ISBN 978 1 78131 895 9
Ebook ISBN 978 1 78131 896 6

10 9 8 7 6 5 4 3 2 1

Design by Paileen Currie

Printed in Singapore